THE KILLING
OF AMERICA

On Our Watch

Frank E. Ahl

PublishAmerica
Baltimore

ISBN: 1-4241-7376-0
PUBLISHED BY PUBLISHAMERICA, LLLP
www.publishamerica.com
Baltimore

Printed in the United States of America

On Our Watch

THE KILLING OF AMERICA

OF AMERICA

The Changing of the Guard

Preface

Exporting American jobs and all phases of our manufacturing to a communist country, China represents the biggest transfer of wealth and power in the history of the world. This book looks at the ramifications of that action and is written as a connect-the-dots book on how it came about and what we can do to correct the situation.

You can watch the Al Gore documentary on global warming to understand how important our pollution problem is. You can see the problems we are now having in funding our Social Security and all other state and federal tax based programs. You can see the price of gasoline and building materials skyrocketing. I am going to show you that all these events stem from the decision to send our jobs abroad. I will also show why the decision to attack Iraq was doomed from the day we invaded that country.

There are books out there that cover one or two of these issues in very one-sided points of view. This book covers all those subjects in a very well rounded look at each issue. I hope you can follow me on this journey. Our future depends on Americans understanding what we have done to ourselves and how our decisions are now affecting the rest of the world.

Thank you PublishAmerica for getting this book to the people.

My family and friends for hanging in for so many years while I created.

Chapters

Introduction

Don't Talk Where You Haven't Walked

When I pick up a book the first thing I do is read the page about the author to see if he has any hands-on experience on the subject he is writing about. Whether I am reading about skydiving or economics I want to read a first hand report of the pitfalls and rewards from the person that lived the experience. I hope you find my credentials to write this book acceptable, but please excuse my writing technique since this is my first book.

This is my background.

I have a four-year college degree with a major in Accounting and a minor in Economics

For 10 years I owned a company that developed, manufactured and marketed a product my son and I invented. We had to deal with the design, materials, production, patents, freight, labels and the hardest part of all dealing with retailers in our attempt to get our product on the market. We saw first hand the pressure to go overseas to get our product made cheaper. This entire process has been the most eye-opening event of my life.

I spent 30 years with the US Government in many capacities. For 18 years I was a US Treasury Agent spending most of that time (15 years) as an IRS Agent auditing all types of businesses. That job allowed me to get a first hand look at every type of business we have in America. It also gave me a chance to understand the US tax codes. For one year I was on assignment to the Federal Wage Price Freeze Program investigating the pricing of goods at retail stores to insure retailers weren't selling products above authorized US Government limits. Wages were also being frozen at that time and I investigated the wages paid by employers to insure wage limit increases were being followed. There were many complaints relating to wages so I also acted as an arbitrator between employers and the employee unions to determine the amount of wage or benefits that was allowed by Federal law. I was assigned to the Federal Energy Administration for 2 years investigating the pricing and production of gas and oil from the oil well to the gas pumps.

For 8 years I was assigned to the Small Business Administration as a loan officer. During that time I audited banks for compliance with SBA lending regulations and also tried to assist small businesses in increasing their bottom line profits. When a business was having problems with their cash flow I would go over their records to identify what went wrong and what they could do to correct the situation. I conducted speeches and seminars on all phases of business operations from profit margins to aging their receivables, analyzing their inventory turnover, sales techniques and looking into everything that effected their cash flow.

My IRS and SBA experience allowed me to really understand the "cause and effect" of reality economics. As I reviewed the accounting books of businesses it would become apparent the decisions the owners were making were going to end up costing more money than they anticipated. Quite often it was too late to help the business because they had made mistakes that were so costly that they would end up going out of business.

At that time I had never owned my own business, but I was starting to get the attitude that I knew all there was to know about running a business. That know-it-all attitude ended when I started my own business. What I had been missing was what it felt like to risk every thing I owned to start my own business and what it felt like to try to overcome the obstacles that a business owner has to deal with daily. It is no easy task dealing with Government regulations, financing, unethical suppliers, finding good help and the difficulty of trying to get your product into retail stores. Taking on this headache without short-term wages or benefits was quite different from my 8 to 5 jobs with the government. The owner of a business only gets paid when the venture itself becomes successful.

I was raised in an area of mining and logging so my entire life has been closely associated with the mining and logging industry. My Granddad and Dad were both miners and both spent part of their work lives working in the logging industry. My Dad had his hand cut off in a saw mill accident which ended his mining career and he spent the rest of his days working at the sawmill driving a forklift. During college I spent one summer working at both a mining operation as a mill worker and as a choke setter dragging logs out of the mountains for a logger. Both jobs are very hard and dirty work, but it also gave me a lot of satisfaction being part of the productivity chain. My other summers during college were spent working on the railroad doing track maintenance.

For 3 years I was in the US Army. I was sent to Germany during the Berlin Crisis of 1961 and remained there until 1964. I was 18 years old when I left and 21 years old when I came back.

I spent 7 months in Gulfport, Mississippi and New Orleans working on the Katrina disaster. The devastation of property and life was certainly comparable to wartime. The difference is that war continues everyday with new destruction, while a storm comes in for just a few hours or days and then makes way for reconstruction. In both cases the killings and destruction is total. After just a few days in Gulfport I wanted to return home, it was hard listening to the stories of people that had lost their loved ones, their neighbors and to see how the storm had destroyed everything they owned. I have always been a compassionate person, but by the time I left the gulf coast my ability to empathize had been taken to a higher level. The loss of lives and property is unavoidable when nature brings this on, it is inexcusable when man does that to man. I saw rich people destroyed as well as the poor. Some of the people spoke in broken English with French or Italian backgrounds, reminding me disasters don't respect nationalities.

By and large the most important ingredient I have in writing this book is my great love of this country. My hope is that by sharing my knowledge we can all better understand what we can do to keep America great.

Chapter 1

Knowing Our Enemy

My very first look at the effects of sending American jobs to another country came in 1994 when I was given the task of conducting a town meeting in a small Western Montana town.

The closing down of the national forest to logging had devastated the area. I was sent in to talk to the local people with the idea of encouraging them to move to other jobs and other locations. Environmentalists had filed suit against the US Forest Service to stop all logging on Federal land in that area. The environmentalists won.

The town's main industry was logging. The mills in the area were being closed. When I got to the meeting I expected to see just a bunch of loggers and mill workers so I was surprised at who showed up at the meeting. The room was packed with loggers and mill workers but also every other business in town was represented from café workers, car salesmen, bankers, and storeowners. A co-worker and myself (I worked for the US Small Business Administration) were the only ones in suits. I started telling them about some of the options that are available to displaced workers, going back to college, going into different trades and those types of remarks. Before I got to far into my speech I got my first interruption from a man in the crowd. His comments really told me what the crowd was thinking and I will repeat his words leaving out a few cuss words.

"You guys really tick me off, you come in here in your suits and high paying jobs and tell us to simply move on with our lives. Do you understand what those damn environmentalists and the damn government has done to our lives? You have shut down an industry that has been this town's livelihood for a hundred years. My granddad and dad worked in the timber here and that is all I know. Your theory about going back to college and changing occupations is a bunch of crap, I never even made it through high school."

His comments then opened the doors for many of the people to express their concern about how a few environmentalists, that had never even been to their town, could file a law suit and stop the sale of timber on the National Forest. There was very little private land in the area so that meant the mills had no option but to close. The other speakers let me know that it was not just the loggers and mill workers affected but every business in that small town was going to be dramatically affected, maybe even too the point of having to close their businesses.

This town was close to the Canadian border so when their mills shut down it provided a boom situation across the border. As time went on the Canadian towns reaped the benefits of logging as they provided the lumber being sold back to the U.S. That little American town still exists but the population continues to decline.

What an eye opener that meeting was to me. From that point on, every time I heard about a mill or factory being shut down I would understand that town's quandary and the despair of each employee and business in the area. It seemed that every day I read about more mills and factories across America closing and the production being transferred to China. I just couldn't believe what I was reading. China? Isn't China a communist country? What are we doing sending our manufacturing to Communist China? I was raised in the 1940's and 1950's when people said the only thing keeping China from being a powerful nation is that it does not have any money.

From 1994 to 2003 the business closings in America became a daily comment in the newspapers as company after company in America sent their manufacturing to China. I kept expecting someone to step up and talk about the insanity of what we were doing. The very core of America was being destroyed. The term globalization was the "buzz" word. Clinton and Gore were actively promoting this concept and excited about America becoming part of this new-world economy. Thomas L. Friedman's books THE WORLD IS FLAT and LEXUS AND THE OLIVE TREE were best sellers. Those books told how great it was to be sending our jobs overseas, Friedman even goes on to say Communism ended when the Berlin Wall came down. I couldn't believe that Americans were buying into this propaganda. This crew went around the world talking to other countries about what our jobs would do for their countries. Globalization was going to be the best thing that ever happened to the world. Neither Clinton nor Friedman looked into one very important thing, what it was going to do to America.

I have never been a person that liked to share my political views but finally in 2003 I could take no more. Someone had to express an opposite opinion from what we were hearing. Sending our jobs overseas could destroy our country and someone had to tell Americans that China was still a communist country. We were feeding the enemy. Our own actions were doing more damage to America than anything terrorists have done to us and no one was saying a word. I finally sat down to write this book in the fall of 2003. I received a hundred rejection letters during the next four years but finally now in 2007 someone is willing to publish my book. I hope as you read this you will forgive my wandering and my repetitiveness and concentrate on the points I am trying to make. My views may differ from yours on Clinton, Gore, Bush, the environment and the Iraq War but I hope you will read the entire book before you make a decision about the case that I am presenting.

We all know about 9-11-01. We all know about terrorist acts around the world and even in America.

This book isn't about either one of those events. There are events taking place in our country right now that are going to be far more destructive to America's well being than any activity already done, or being contemplated by any terrorist. That is what this story is about, our real greatest enemy.

Imagine a plot by our worst enemy that includes taking away all our money, all our jobs, and our entire tax base so we can't afford the great armies and government machinery we have grown accustomed to. The enemy closes our factories, shuts down our mills, and puts millions of our people out of work. Now imagine that we let this enemy do all this damage to America and no one even raises an eyebrow. That would be like a real life horror film, wouldn't it? It is happening as we speak. The enemy I am talking about is the American people ourselves, in whatever capacity we fill, elected official, corporate leader, government worker, business owner, educator, union official and of course the American consumer.

Most people recognize something is amiss in America but they are not quite sure what it is. They themselves, or a friend or relative are out of a job and they know the newspapers are still blaming 9-11. The government is telling us everything is fine and recovery is on the way.

Economics is not an exact science but it is certainly very predictable. If you tinker with one thing it will effect a lot of other things. Who has been tinkering with our economy? How can we stop the decline that is happening? Can our greatest enemy be ourselves sending of our jobs overseas?

To solve a problem, we must first recognize that there is a problem, then be willing to act on our findings. You and I know the economy of America is starting to show signs of stress and there doesn't seem to be enough attention being paid to solving the situation. This book will go into some details that will hopefully point us in a direction of addressing the problems.

In the last 10 years, hundreds of thousands of manufacturing jobs have been sent overseas and we are now starting to outsource office jobs to other countries. A strong national economy is usually based on a strong manufacturing structure so why would America voluntarily ship so many of its jobs overseas? A lot of forces came into play, from the government, big businesses, environmentalists, unions, and the American consumer. We will look at all of them.

I have tried to devote a separate chapter to each of the elements that appear to have led to our declining economy. No matter what your beliefs are you will find some chapters that will embrace your beliefs and some chapters that will go against your personal views. This is good because more than anything, I want this book to make people start thinking. We should all think about the complete consequences to every action we take and remember most people's views are arrived at by looking at just one side of the story. I hope this book will help you look at all sides of our decision making process.

Chapter 2

Understanding Reality Economics

A bad economy can destroy a life, a family, a business, and a government and even bring a country to its knees. Whether we are a business or an individual, our economic situation is brought on by our decisions, usually overspending, but in America's case it is mainly about giving away our jobs. The actions taken by our elected officials, businesses, unions and environmentalists have all contributed to what I call "the killing of America". Many of the people involved simply don't understand reality economics and the cause and effect of the decisions they make.

This book will attempt to bring everyone to the same table, no matter where you are in the food chain, from a single mother trying to survive to a large corporation trying to get their share of the pie. This book also includes information for our public officials and public servants. In a time of crisis, no one is exempt. We all have to look hard at what's happening and make changes before our situation worsens.

Historically, strong economies are related to a course of events that start with raw materials and go through the process of changing those raw materials into consumer goods that end up at a retail store. At each stage of this transformation from raw materials to the end product there is a value-added stop. Value-added is a phrase that means each time something is changed it becomes more valuable. An example would be turning a ton of ore into 10 pounds of gold or turning a tree into a living room table and chairs. Any raw material may make a dozen value-added stops before it is turned into a consumer product and ends up on a retail shelf.

I will start with some basic economic laws but will get much more specific as the book goes on. We can start by looking at a very simple renewable resource, the basic tree, and see where that tree might lead us. The tree must first be identified as one that is ready to harvest, that job is done by a forest service employee or an individual hired by the landowner or sawmill. The tree must be cut down and skidded to a loading location. The tree is put onto a truck and shipped to the sawmill. At the sawmill a skid operator unloads the tree and sends it to the cutting operation to make lumber or pulp.

When the lumber comes out of the mill it is shipped to another company that will turn the wood into furniture, paper, plywood etc and the value of that wood product increases at each step of the operation. Whatever direction it goes there will be employees there, walking the raw material through the next course to turn it into something that is saleable.

As you can see the simple event of cutting down a tree has created many jobs at the location where the tree is cut and where the wood is converted into usable goods. Also, at each location there are secondary jobs being created to help that individual doing the actual work on the tree. That worker is buying gas at a local store, work boots, safety equipment and he is buying a pickup to get to work. Someone else is making each of the items he is buying and that person is also creating their own food chain. In short each job is helping the entire community survive and prosper and is helping the economy of the county, state and country where the business activity is taking place.

In our example each value-added location created jobs for everyone around, the worker and those who service him. Also, each time money changes hands in this process of value-added productivity, taxes are being paid. Those taxes support the local schools, teachers are being paid, county officials are being paid and some of the taxes go into the Federal coffers to run our government. Taxes are being paid into social security and unemployment compensation, Police forces are paid and even money to support our U.S. military comes out of the taxes paid during this manufacturing operation.

The lower you are on the food chain the more you understand this concept of value-added and jobs-create-jobs. People that have physical jobs like manufacturing or construction know that their job depends on so many other businesses and workers. They must rely on the shipments of raw materials or parts from some other company and each position is just a step in the value-added chain.

When you eliminate that value-added chain, everything is interrupted, right down to the waitress at the corner café who depends on those workers to come in for coffee or lunch. In our example of a log mill operating in a small town, if you shut the mill down it can literally shut down the entire community. When the timber workers have to leave town in search of work all the supporting businesses are greatly effected. Those supporting businesses themselves may have to close.

The above example isn't an economic theory it is economic reality. In logging areas around America, lumber mills are being shut down while more and more lumber comes into the US from Canada. Some people have the mind set that bringing in wood from Canada is OK because it helps our environment. That concept will be further discussed when I get to the chapter on environmentalists.

This jobs-create-jobs concept is at all levels of production. My example was set in a small logging town, but that same occurrence happens anywhere raw goods are being processed or manufacturing is taking place. Looking at products that are made from metals, you can follow those same principles all the way from mining the ore to the finished paper clip you have on your desk.

One area I am very familiar with and dealt with for years is the plastics industry. It is almost impossible to compete with a place like China when their average wage is sixty cents an hour compared to US workers averaging about $12 an hour. But as we have noted above that $.60 per hour wage earner in China making our plastic parts is only the tip of the iceberg. If that job were in the US that $12 an hour wage earner would be helping to support many storekeepers and sending tax dollars into our government not the China government.

I don't want to belabor the importance of a manufacturing economy but it is the single most important item you will have in a thriving economy. Some economic theorists and government leaders believe America is past the days of blue-collar workers and manufacturing and we will discuss that thought process later.

What has made the US different from other countries around the world? Why have we prospered so well while other countries haven't moved and still have third world status? Most of those other countries never moved up to become manufacturing nations. Those countries may have as much natural wealth, gold, ore, timber and oil as we do so why was the US able to accomplish so much? Certainly one of the reasons is that those countries didn't move forward is that they didn't develop their own natural resources. America made the blueprint on how to develop natural resources and by manufacturing turn them into valuable commodities to provide for our own needs and to sell the excess around the world.

Another important asset America has is the quality of our workers and our citizens. We live in a country where we respect other peoples right to religion, their color and their educational background. We have jobs for all levels and abilities of our population. We have never been a country that had much fighting between factions so we all work for an end goal. We create jobs, we work hard at our jobs, and we have become a people that are generous with our excess. Helping others has always been a way of life for Americans.

We are also a country that uses our natural resources, our oil, ore, coal, timber and the crops we grow. In a lot of cases we may have extracted our natural resources in a way that did damage to our streams or environment but as years went on we got better and became more conscious of our surroundings. Most people are aware of what it means to be in charge of things; well we are in charge of our own natural resources. If we shut down our natural resources and stop mining or logging we have stopped the very first event that is needed to be a manufacturing nation.

We now are all on the same page as to what generates a strong economy. Jobs. Yes indeed, it is jobs. But all jobs are not created equal. As noted above, the jobs we were describing were jobs relating to creating goods for our use, goods that are made from our natural resources. Some people forget that every thing we touch, wood, plastic or metal has to be either grown, mined or refined.

The more you shut down a country's natural resources, the more that country's economy is lost. If we don't tap into our natural resources we lose jobs, good jobs, value-added jobs, jobs that allow us to live as a successful developed nation. It is in fact one of the things that separates us from 3rd world countries. A decision to not utilize our natural resources is the first step in the destruction of our country's economy. As we have seen, countries that don't utilize their natural resources remain 3rd world countries. We are now witnessing what happens to a great country that opts to discontinue utilizing their own natural resources and instead ships all that productivity to other countries. We are watching China grow while America is going backwards.

One of our leaders (Bill Clinton) stated a few years ago that we will become a nation exporting technology and we will become a service country. Do you think that man, our leader, understood reality economics? Lets look at service jobs and you decide if it is a good trade off to let other countries do the manufacturing with our technology. What is it we are supposed to service? All public servants are servicing our needs to operate our schools, staff our libraries, and protect us at both the local and national level by our police and military. But remember there is no value-added to their work in the truest sense. These jobs take money out of our public funds but most of those jobs don't contribute to putting money back into our public coffers. The economy must be strong if we are to hire a sufficient number of these public servants and we have to be bringing in a lot of taxes elsewhere to afford those public servants.

An office working job, no matter how many papers are scuffled in a day, does not create the same value-added product at the end of his day that a person does that works in the industry making goods. Quite often office workers look down on those who come home dirty from creating the very goods we require to live. It is easy to see why even some of our leaders think we can send our manufacturing overseas when they think Americans no longer need those low class jobs. People with that thought process don't understand the multiplying effect of jobs and they don't understand reality economics.

Historically, service jobs were created to assist the worker who is producing goods for us to live like food, clothing, tools, and transportation. Now more and more of those types of jobs are being filled overseas. That entire food chain of productivity is being given away to other countries. Now our goods come to America from overseas and are put on a truck or railcar and sent directly to retail store like Wal-Mart. All those other fine jobs that should have existed in this manufacturing chain no longer exist in the U.S.

I think by now you understand what reality economics looks like. It is a beautiful thing when it is all working. Until the 1990's that is what the U.S. looked like, a country full of miners, loggers, manufacturers, factory workers, making clothing, shoes, and cars. This created the greatest country in the world, with one of the highest standards of living anywhere in the world.

So much for the nice stuff. Now let's get down to the real meat and potatoes of this book. Someone is killing America. What happened to the American dream of having a meaningful job producing our own consumer goods, the goods we wear and touch and drive? Some may think those jobs can be replaced by computer jobs, after all we are in the dot.com era. Now that you understand the value-added jobs create jobs scenario, replacing those manufacturing jobs with computer jobs just isn't a fair tradeoff is it? Americans are consumers; we can't consume anything the computer gives us. Our standard of living depends on us getting consumer goods.

Every thing you do in an economic system has more ripple effects than most of our leaders understand. When we gave away our jobs, we also gave away making new factories. I understand places like Shanghai, China now have mile after mile of new factories while the factories in the U.S. are getting old, run down and a lot of them are closing. China is buying up the steel from around the world, for it's own use and for sale back to the U.S. Our steel factories have been pretty much shut down. The price of steel is skyrocketing in the U.S. Do you think that makes the U.S. vulnerable? If America has a crisis or has a falling out with China, where does that put us?

In the early 1990's one of the biggest gaps between economic theory and economic reality emerged, something called "Globalization". The idea was to open up all the countries of the world to trade and manufacturing. The invention of the cell phones and computers would let even 3rd world countries come to the world trade table. The poor countries of the world would finally be able to share in the abundance of the good life. I love this theory, my heart goes out to the poor and the starving and the uneducated, no matter where they live. This is a something

I have always wished for, no more wars, no more hunger, finally everyone in the world would be brought up to a higher level so they can reach their potential.

When I first heard of globalization, I assumed that it would mean each country that bought into the idea of globalization would start developing their own economy. They would start by utilizing their own natural resources, building factories to make the consumer products their country's population needed and develop their agriculture to the level that is available in the 21st Century. All this would result in a higher standard of living for all those countries that embraced this globalization idea. After all we all live in one big world that was certainly made smaller by the new computer age. Great theory!

But here is the catch, the people organizing this globalization concept didn't understand how economics work so what came about in reality wasn't at all what I had envisioned. The people that implemented this grand concept never intended that each country would help themselves with their own manufacturing and creating their own jobs. In reality those people involved had a vision that the best and quickest way to bring prosperity to those countries was to transfer all the jobs they needed from America. Those countries will be given all of Americas manufacturing and America can just buy back those goods they make. They thought America no longer needed those menial manufacturing jobs because we were at the head of the computer age. They also thought we were a very rich nation and we could afford to let poorer countries in on our prosperity. (The "They" I am talking about are people like Clinton, Gore, Friedman and all the foreign leaders that they went around the world talking to.)

When I saw that the globalization concept didn't include requiring those countries to improve their own lot, but rather take away Americas jobs, I knew what was about to happen to America. I had spent my career dealing with the consequences of businesses making poor judgement calls and there was no doubt in my mind that this whole idea was going to be a train wreck for America. To close down America's natural resources and factories and send it all overseas was without a doubt the most insane economic decision I had ever heard of. I have seen hundreds of businesses go out of business because of bad decisions but this is America, an entire country, and we were making the worst economic decision in American history.

It is hard to believe that a concept so inviting could turn out to be the most destructive event in American history. To understand just how big a problem America now faces go into Wal-Mart and pick up 20 items in each of the departments and see how many items are made in the USA. Pick up a shirt, shoes, socks, toys, you name it and I doubt if you will find a single item with a Made-in-USA sticker. When you look at those products remember the value-added food chain that is now being fed in China. From processing the raw materials to the actual making of the goods, many families in foreign countries are reaping the benefits. Instead of the U.S. government getting all those taxes, we are feeding a government (mainly Communist China) that we don't trust. Does that bring a tear to your eyes? What will you tell your kids and grandkids when they don't have jobs? Will you tell them you allowed this to happen without even putting up a fight?

Chapter 3

The Government

I want to retrace America's steps for the last few decades and try to find out what went wrong. How did we get to the point that we have shut down our natural resources and sent so much of our manufacturing out of country? It appears a logical place to start, is with our Federal Government.

From what I can find, and remember is that in the 1990's President Clinton took up the cause for Globalization with the idea that the US should open its economic doors to as many countries as possible and make it easier for them to import goods into the US. We may never know whether that Globalization concept came from him or one of his economic advisors. What we do know is that the big push to include almost the entire world in making consumer goods for America went on to become a monster that gobbled up American jobs.

The politician's thought it sounded good and big business thought it sounded good. Right from the start the average American didn't like the idea of what was about to happen. Ross Pero said it best when he was running for president "If the North American Fair Trade Act is approved the only sound you will hear is the sound of U.S. jobs and U.S. money being sucked out of this country". That consequence appears to be the same no matter what country we sent our jobs to.

There were stories floating around that both big business and foreign countries were being given a lot of our elected leaders ear in exchange for contributions to their reelection campaigns. This so-called soft money looks to an average American like a bribe.

The Clinton Administration set a new low in the standards of receiving money, but that is just the way politics works. Our Senators and Congressmen do the same thing. Why do we as Americans allow that? Are they not all our 'public servants'? This is one of the many things I hope we can change.

Maybe we can change the system by not allowing any foreign country, or foreign group to give any elected, appointed, or hired Government employee anything. No cash payments, no trips, no gifts, in other words treat them all as if they are a normal government worker (they are not allowed to receive anything from outside sources).

Regarding the contributions that are given by big businesses, individuals, special interest groups, or any other contribution to the political system, how about sticking all those funds into a single place. A coffer for the party involved, a bank for the democrats another for the republicans. No one is allowed to know who put the money in so, when a person is elected he does not know who contributed what, so he owes no one favors. The only favors he owes are to the American people; he has to do what is best for America as a whole.

When we, as a country, were rich we hired a lot of servants like we were rich kings. We built castles (new Federal Buildings) for our servants in every town. Now we even hire guards to guard those building and our servants. We give our servants the best wages, benefits, and retirement systems that our money can buy. We thought they were looking out for us, the American people, the American way of life.

Now we discover they were not looking out for us after all. What can we do as a country to bring back our prosperity? We are no longer rich; we have given away our jobs and our future. Every day more and more jobs are going overseas. Our leaders decisions are bankrupting America.

Around the world Americans have been getting a lot of bad press because our government makes bad decisions. Our leaders think they know what is best for each country and what is best for the world, but they don't seem to know what is best for America. Why is that?

Bush and a few of his close advisors decided to invade Iraq based on a single intelligence report that Iraq may have weapons of mass destruction. For the first time in America's history we invaded a country that wasn't invading another country. We did the very thing we have always hated. We did it without a thought about the consequences. Anyone who has ever spent time in the Middle East (or any other foreign country) knows that those people are far different from Americans. They have different religions, a completely different way of life. Their life styles and differences have been in existence for thousands of years.

It is becoming more evident every day that the action our government is taking does not reflect the attitude of the average American. We are a people that love to provide for our families and we love to share any extra we have. We are not an aggressive people like most of the world is starting to view us. We are hard working and want to have a future for our children. All this is being threatened by the way our government is conducting business. Many of us have written our congressmen asking them to stop exporting our jobs but so far no one in Washington is listening. Their response is that their top economic advisors are saying the economy is doing great.

Our leaders apparently thought by letting China do all our manufacturing that they would become a better country, a country of capitalists who would spread that new wealth among their poor people. All this was going to make China treat their people better etc etc. But, no matter what anyone says, they are still a communist country and as far as helping the poor our first obligation should be to help our own poor.

The American people are being misled by this entire concept. What is best for America, in the long run, will be best for the rest of the world. Is it too late to get our jobs back, our factories back, and our integrity back? No, it is not too late but something has to be done soon. America is no longer the big fat cat country that can put people in office to spend our money like there is no end to it. We are no longer a rich king nation. When someone is rich they hire a lot of servants, when they lose their wealth the first thing to go are the servants.

The government system in place is so big and our public servants so entrenched, it will be hard to get them out, but we have to. We have to change our way of thinking. We have to look at every elected official to see if he possesses wisdom. We have to look at the credentials of those we elect. Don't just look at their education, people like attorneys, educators, government workers, and economists sometimes lack the deep understanding of what makes an economy run.

The new-age elected official needs to be someone that puts the interest of the average American above anyone else, above minority groups or special interest groups, and above helping any other country at the expense of America. He needs to be someone that is willing to forgo pork barrel spending and will limit his spending to items that help all of America. He will investigate each Federal agency to decide if it is really needed.

That new-age official will understand that he is a public servant and will conduct himself accordingly. He will not accept any money or favors from anyone. He will take only what the American people give him for wages. In short he will truly do what is best for America. He will never vote in favor of invading another country unless that country invades another country. He will vote to change the import laws and immigration laws or any other laws that will help America.

He will understand that his purpose as an employee is first protecting America, its people and ideals. He will do his best to study all sides of an issue before he makes a judgement call on major issues. Did I mention he would never accept a penny or a gift from any country or individual as long as he is a public servant? He will understand that the king (America) he is working for is no longer rich, with unlimited funds.

The decisions he will make will be tough, especially tough on those countries we have given our manufacturing and jobs to. He has to remember that his job is to give Americans back their jobs. He must be willing to totally reverse the attitude we have about giving away all our jobs to benefit globalization. He must understand that America does not owe Communist China the right to manufacture all our consumer goods.

He must understand that based on our current economic situation we may have to close our borders to any more immigration until we can sort out what we should be doing. He must understand that America is a place that really can't take on all the worlds poor. He will understand that America doesn't have the right to force other countries into becoming capitalistic or democratic.

He will work hard to try and understand what it is the average American wants. The average American wants his job back and is tired of seeing our public servants making such bad decisions on their dealings with other countries. Americans are tired of seeing billions of dollars being sent to other countries while our own public health system is a mess. The poverty in our streets is growing. Our prison population is the highest in history. Crime comes with poverty and the average American deserves better.

The new era public servant will understand that the answer to using our natural resources is not to shut them down but to work on ways to use them more efficiently with less damage to our environment. He will respect the intent of our founding fathers to respect each citizen of America and will not be a part of pushing some special interest groups opinion onto our population.

Once we understand how the system works we can be more informed citizens and we can start voicing our opinions to our elected officials. It is a slow process but it will come about. We are just starting to see the effect of sending our jobs overseas and in the very near future even our elected officials will understand that as the U.S. debt grows. We can't keep reducing our tax revenues because of lost jobs and lost manufacturing and survive at the rate our government spends.

Chapter 4

Manufacturing

Americans have spent their lives going into stores and getting whatever they want. Every thing we can possibly desire from clothing to sporting goods to toys and furniture. As consumers we never gave much thought about where it comes from or how it got to the store. Our concern has never been where-was-it-made or how many people it took to make it. Our only concern was whether or not we had enough money to buy it.

When the economy was booming, we didn't even pay attention to price, we were shoppers who were accustomed to buying what we wanted. But as the economy got tighter pricing began to become more of an issue. We started judging our purchases more and more by price. For years there have been a few products made overseas that were dramatically less expensive but the quality of the product was also very inferior. Early Japanese and Mexican products were mainly purchased by poorer people who couldn't afford the Made in the USA products.

In the past the American brands were all made here in the US. That is no longer the case, brand names like Nike, Fruit of the Loom, etc are now mainly made overseas. Based on our early experiences with foreign made products those items made overseas should be priced extremely cheap, but that is no longer the case. They are priced so high one would assume they are made in the USA. We are paying premium for name brands that used to be made in the USA but are now made in China or other countries, mainly along the Pacific Rim.

New Balance is a shoe still made in the USA that is comparable to the foreign-made Nike brand. The New Balance is priced less then its foreign rival. Why is that? There are many reasons, name recognition, advertising, product design and acceptance. Nike is well known as a company that gets cheap overseas labor while still charging premium prices for their products. Why do they do business like that? The answer is of course because they can.

Nike is no different from all the other companies that make our consumer products; the company wants to maximize their profits. The American buyer should be offended by this practice of charging made in USA prices for goods made in China and refuse to buy them.

The manufacturers that have this practice want our business, but do not want to support America and the American buyer. It is strictly a one-way street. What can the American worker do about this grave inequity? The most important thing he can do is simply put back on the shelf any item not made in the USA. Do without if you have to. If you are a shareholder in a company that has switched its manufacturing overseas write the company expressing your opinion that you want their product to again be made in the USA. If you are really committed to this idea sell your stock in those companies.

To understand why a company abandons America to give foreign workers the jobs we must take a look at the overall manufacturing industry in America. What made it change so dramatically? Greed, union pressure, environmental issues, pressures from retail stores; indifferent buying public and government regulations and taxes all played a part.

Before it became a matter of pure greed there were a lot of events taking place within the American manufacturing world that foreshadowed the events leading up to closing the US factories and going overseas.

Union problems and environmental issues will have their own chapters in this book so only a short look will be made now at those issues. We will look now at those issues from the viewpoint of the manufacturer.

The union members were like every other phase of the U.S.; they wanted a standard of living to go along with living in the greatest consumer country in the world. The union members expected annual wage increase, more benefits like medical and retirement, more sick and annual leave, all of these things that cost the manufacturer money. When you added up the cost of all these items the hourly wages were getting up into the ranges of $20, $30, and maybe even $40 per hour. Added to that was higher and higher workers compensation and unemployment tax rates. Unions would strike when their demands weren't met so more companies were becoming dissatisfied with the cost of the American worker.

During this same time the environmentalists were making it harder to both manufacture goods and to get the actual raw materials. Demands were being made on the companies to improve their pollution standards. Environmental issues were putting pressure on old factories to clean up their pollution. These companies were looking at huge retooling costs to make those improvements.

Factories were becoming outdated and in need of repair or replacement. Competition was becoming keener and the shareholders were expecting a better return on their dollar. The dot.com era of quick return on your investment and large profits were becoming something manufacturers and their investors wanted. Companies watched as their competition started going overseas and saw the profits those companies were making escalate. Stock in those companies going overseas rapidly went up in value as soon as it became known they were moving their production.

At about this same time the Federal Government started getting active in wanting to include more and more of the world in the good life of free enterprise and capitalism. The North American Free Trade Act wanted to open the doors to Canada and Mexico to allow an ease of imports. The U.S. became active in trying to get China and other countries involved in the free trade idea, hoping that globalization would be beneficial to us all.

Where the connection was made between big business and the US Government is not known. What is known is that the government's push to open up imports from other countries was a tremendous help to business. Big business finally had an escape to get away from the problems being presented by the unions, the environmentalists, government taxes and aging manufacturing facilities while at the same increasing the profits for the company by astronomical proportions.

In a period of less then 10 years the fate of the American worker, and the American economy had been sealed. The idea of how great "Globalization" could be was going to be put to the test. Our government leaders and economic advisors thought the US could be a country that could survive as an exporter of technology. Those same people thought by helping 3rd world countries become more capitalistic they would also become more democratic and it would all add up to a big happy world.

Businesses were more than happy to abandon their old factories, the pesky union demands, the environmentalists and all the while they could see the bottom-line profits go to unbelievable highs. To show you what a big deal it was to do away with the American worker, here is a real example of the difference in wage cost between countries. In Spokane, Washington, USA the average production line employee in a plastics operation cost the company $12.50 per hour. That same company has a plant in Mexico where a similar worker gets

$2.50 per hour. Again that same company has a plant in China and pays $.50 per hour for doing the same job.

Isn't that amazing, the cost per item of anything they make in China is far less, so think of the amazing amount of profit for the manufacturer. It seems like a golden calf doesn't it? And the big thing is most of the savings go into the pockets of the company's top brass wages and into the return of the shareholder, the savings is seldom passed on to the American consumer.

You thought that the idea of reducing the cost of manufacturing should lead to a lower retail cost to the consumer. The consumer may have saved a little bit but for the most part the prices didn't go down much. Pick up a pair of Nike shoes made in China and think back a few years ago when they were made in the USA, there isn't much difference.

So much for the past. We can all see why the manufacturer went overseas but now lets look at today. Where do we go from here? We don't need a crystal ball; the writing is all over the wall. The cause and effect of our decisions are unbelievable; the USA is being devastated by the above actions.

The entire trend in manufacturing is what the business leaders view as a "no-brainer", send as much of the manufacturing overseas as possible. Management in most plants in the nation proudly state that they have personal connections to China where they can produce anything a customer orders. They boast that China can do it quicker, cheaper, and better than the US.

Most manufacturers today think this scenario is the way to go, just ship it overseas and eliminate a lot of hassles. Every phase of the manufacturing is taken care of and all they have to do is concentrate on the marketing.

The little company that I personally owned was so small that it really didn't make a difference where I built my product but it meant a lot to me, I love the USA. I loved to go to the little companies here in the USA that were making my various parts. I loved the fact that they appreciated that I insisted that my product be made in the USA. Maybe most of all, I understood the importance of keeping the manufacturing in the USA. I understood the cause and effect of any decision to abandon our American production. I know that the USA is not rich enough to survive the continued deterioration of our manufacturing industry. Bottom line, I love America and wouldn't do anything to hinder this way of life so I opted to keep all production in the US. I have now licensed my product to another company and I hope they continue to make it here in the good old USA.

As we speak China (and other countries but mainly China) are busy building mile after mile of new factories while in America we are building very few new plants. Our factories are becoming obsolete and being shut down. In American manufacturing we used to use our own natural resources to build our products, be it metals, woods, or plastics, but now all those products are being milled at locations outside the USA. Now at every phase of the manufacturing operation, from the iron ore or timber all the way through the finished products, there are millions of workers being employed in China to make American goods. No doubt taxes are paid at every level of production in the manufacturing process, not to the US Government but to the Communist China Government. Is it possible that many of those factories are owned by the Chinese government? I don't know, but we know for sure that the ruling Communist Party will get its share.

Anyone who thinks the doing away with our natural resource development/manufacturing structure will have only a minimum effect on our society is gravely mistaken. Office workers, government workers and educators have a tendency to underestimate the importance of our blue-collar workforce.

All the things that we enjoy, from our standard of living, to the things provided for us by our government and our independence from any other country are all things we have taken a lot of pride in. In the past we knew we were strong enough to support our life styles, that could come to an end. I hate to be the bearer of bad news but the next few years are critical to our continued standard of living. Yes manufacturing is that important to this country.

Do we really intend to have China become strong by giving them more and more of our manufacturing jobs? Do we understand the long-range effect of this move? Do we understand that the giving away of our manufacturing jobs affects us all?

We all have to be concerned. When you read about another 1,000 manufacturing jobs being sent overseas remember that will have a direct effect on 5,000 other workers. How do you feel about that? Do you go along with the concept that those workers that lost their jobs had better buck-up and change occupations because of this new age of globalization? Or do you think we should bring their jobs back from overseas?

This cause and effects relating to manufacturing jobs isn't just theory, this is reality economics. For our leaders to think those misplaced workers will simply have to change their occupation is so misleading. There is no place else they can work where their efforts can bring so much to our economy.

There has been lot of talk about how we will become a country exporting technology. You only export technology once. The country you send the technology to will send you back the fruits of that technology by the next boat, in the form of consumer goods. It is a well documented fact that most inventions come from the United States, but once it is invented it can be made by any country who has set themselves up as a manufacturing nation. They can do it cheaper and just as good as the USA.

So what can we do as individuals? The government has its own momentum and continually tries to open more doors with the feeling that the doors they open are two way, other countries will buy from us and we will buy from them. We are just now getting the statistics together to show hundreds of billions of dollars more is being spent each year to buy back our consumer goods than those countries are spending buying US goods.

Historically, during a time of war our factories are turned to the manufacture of war goods but America has become a country with fewer and fewer manufacturing facilities if that need arises.

The manufacturing companies themselves think they have found the fattened golden calf, the goose that lays the golden egg, the fountain of endless profits with fewer headaches than they ever dreamed they would have. They are not about to back off from their fixation of sending it all overseas. Profits, profits, and more profits and bigger and bigger wages for the top brass.

Manufacturers have to be made to understand that we are fighting an economic war that they think they are winning with this off shore manufacturing but in fact it is killing the USA. These temporary gains are at the expense of America, the very country that made it all possible. Their customers are US citizens that will become less and less able to buy their "off shore" goods.

It is going to be hard to wean manufacturers from the cheap labor, but it has to be done. If we view this economic event truly as the war it is then it would be easier for us all to do our part to solve the problem. In war you are either a friend or foe. Companies exporting our manufacturing are definitely not our friends.

Each one who believes in the American system of taking care of US citizens before we take care of the rest of the world can make a difference. We are the consumers of those goods coming in from the Pacific Rim, off shore, overseas, out of country, however you want to politely call it. If we don't buy those goods they will stop coming into our country.

Every time we shop we have a chance to vote whether or not we agree with the system. Just lay that product back down and look for something similar made in the USA. Write the companies that are making those products and tell them you no longer want to continue to buy their goods if they will not make them in the USA.

It isn't just the manufacturing of goods; it is now "outsourcing" of jobs requiring someone working with the telephone or computers that have the same effect. Dell Computers recently shipped a lot of their office jobs to India and the customers were not happy. A lot of people wrote Dell and complained. Dell has agreed to return those jobs back to the USA. We can make a difference. In a later chapter I mention some of the companies that are outsourcing their telephone and computer work.

The most important thing a company can do is to please its customers. Manufacturers need to remember that the American buyer is their customer, not their investors nor China.

Chapter 5

Unions

We are all very familiar with Unions. They have a long and checkered past. Some of their leaders misused funds but the unions themselves did a lot for America. Some people feel that the union's time has passed, and maybe it has, but maybe they are like the rest of us, they simply have to change.

The unions brought a lot to our table as far as productivity, safety and job security. They certainly added to the overall picture of growth, quality of goods and services and for that, we must forever be thankful.

But that was yesterday. In today's climate when you upset management it is certainly possible they will simply eliminate your job and send it overseas. Union members have to be willing to accept more changes in their work place to allow for the latest improvements in production capabilities. It is not the time to be fighting over an occasional lost position due to technology. In short the union has been just one more thorn in the side of management that made closing a factory and taking production overseas so desirable.

There is no group of Americans that love the "Made in the USA" label more then union members. They were fighting the issue of overseas manufacturing long before the rest of us even thought about it. They knew first hand the effects of any product being taken out of US production and the ripple effect it has on all the other jobs.

As you read this book and you wonder just how devastating it is on our economy to send our manufacturing overseas, talk to any union member that has been involved in manufacturing, he will have his own stories of how bad it is. They have seen communities and even entire towns changed when manufacturing jobs leave the area. They have seen the personal destruction job losses have caused to the individuals involved. Bankruptcy, divorce, families separated as they look for work and even suicide.

Union members have to change their thought process because they are no longer in the driver seat but it doesn't mean they have to go away. The unions were a vital part of our past and can be a constructive part of the changes we now need to make.

When manufacturers considered moving the operations overseas it gave them the ability to walk away from their union problems. That was one more headache they no longer had to deal with and the bonus was, it saved them a lot of money in wages and benefits. Let's get the unions and the manufacturers back together. We know that could be one more stumbling block we can overcome.

Chapter 6

Consumers

By now you have probably guessed where this story is going. It all comes back to the consumer. The manufacturing that is being done overseas involves a lot of the everyday consumer goods you pick up at stores like Wal-Mart. Where those goods are made should make a difference to you, the consumer. Now that you understand the jobs create jobs idea and value added concept would you rather see jobs for yourself here in the US or would you rather have them done in some foreign country like China.

In good times, the average American might say "well it is good to provide jobs for the poor around the world". I agree with this heart-felt feeling, people need jobs to support their families no matter what country they live in. But the reality is that if the giving away of our jobs creates major problems within my own country then I vote against it.

Our concern is certainly for all the worlds' people but it is very wrong to ask the average citizen to give up his job and lower his standard of living to provide a job to a people he has no obligation to. So what are we going to do about it? Big companies and big government are not looking out for our well being and nothing will change until we make our feelings known. America is the best place in the world, lets keep it that way.

The average American didn't even know the government, big business and foreign countries were coming up with a grand globalization concept. Had we been informed about it we would have screamed at that time before it grew to be such a devastating event. One thing for sure is we now see that America is not big enough and rich enough to bring the rest of the world up to our standards, but the giving away of our jobs can bring us down to their standard of living.

America, please, for the sake of our children and grandchildren stand up and fight for this life we have worked so hard to achieve. We earned the right to manufacture our own goods and develop our own natural resources. No other country earned that right. What did China do to earn that right?

Every time you pull a dollar out of your billfold or purse and spend it on an American product you are placing your vote. Also every time you put a product back on the shelf that is made out of country you are voting against the company who thought they could fire US workers and still sell us goods. We need a national "don't buy foreign goods month".

I don't believe that the government or our leaders can change this situation of all our products being made overseas, but there is one organization that has the power to change this. That organization is WAL-MART. They too are a buyer, the biggest buyer in the world and they can make things happen. They have the power to have their suppliers (vendors) do anything they demand. If WAL-MART told every one of their suppliers that effective in one year they would only sell made-in-America products I guarantee you that the vendors will comply. That store calls all the shots to their vendors and I have never heard of one vendor not complying with their wishes. If they don't comply, Wal-Mart simple will not buy products from them. Does Wal-Mart love America and its customers enough to take this action? We will see.

Wal-Mart might argue that their cost will go up, but they shouldn't go up much. The profits of the vendors bringing goods in from overseas will go down but they will still be able to turn a profit, but just not as astronomical as they are used to.

I have been a vendor and had my product in stores so I know how it works. When I got my product into Costco I had to jump through a lot of hoops and if I didn't comply there were a lot of other vendors that were ready to take my place.

I understand that in Germany, the government has required manufacturers to make at least 25% of their product in Germany. That approach would work in the US but it would take a lot to pull that off. Big companies would not tolerate that action and the way our elected officials conduct business I don't think we would ever be able to pass laws requiring that action. But Wal-Mart is another story; if the owners would do that, it would be a done deal.

Chapter 7

Big Box Stores (National Chains)

Big Box Stores and big national chains are another player in this whole dilemma giving away U.S. jobs and letting other countries just "take over" our manufacturing. Some people view the Wal-Mart, Costco, Lowes, Menards and Home Depot as a real friend of the consumer. They all try to price lower than anyone else around. Certainly other locally owned stores can not even pretend to compete with the prices found in the Big Box Stores and national chains.

Lets look at some of the tactics of these Big Box stores and see what they do that may be adding fuel to the foreign buying fire. The best and most public example is of course Wal-Mart, which has become the biggest Retail Company in the world. They are known for being extremely tough on their suppliers/vendors. Some consider their hard attitude just a sign of doing smart business and as such, it promotes low prices to the buyers.

As big as Wal-Mart is, they have no inventory storage problem because the vendor is notified that the goods being ordered have to be at the store on a particular date (called just in time drop shipment). The goods aren't being shipped from a Wal-Mart warehouse because they have no storage facility other than the store itself. Stories abound as to how long the vendor then has to wait before he is paid for the goods, but apparently

90 days is the norm. Most locally owned stores have only up to 30 days to pay their vendors for the inventory.

Home Depot is known for charging its vendors for shelf space in their stores. Some suppliers pay millions of dollars for their prime space in Home Depot. I suspect this is another tactic that other big box stores also use.

Costco has a policy of asking the vendor how much they have invested in their product and that is what they will pay the vendor for the product. If the vendor wants to have any profit margin they must go back and get the price reduced from their sources and one of the best ways is to take the product overseas. Costco does have some polices that make up for their low prices paid to the vender. They pay the vendor in full for their goods in less then 30 days after the goods are picked up. Costco picks up the product at your factory so the vendor pays no freight. Most Costco items are placed on pallets by the vendors so there are very few items that need store clerk handling. Costco is also well known for treating their employees very good so there is very little employee turnover. The president of Costco started the company and draws a small wage compared to any other company of its kind.

None of these things sound too bad do they? It is certainly evident why other local stores can't compete with those stores head on. Their buying power is so phenomenal that vendors are waiting in line to get a chance to place their goods into those stores.

These Big Box stores have long shopping hours, open early and stay open late at night. In short they seem to meet all the needs of the consumer, lower prices, better selection, and they are open more convenient hours. So what is the problem and why are they being blamed for part of our economic crisis?

Big Box stores try to take all the credit for cheap prices but in fact a lot of the savings come out of the pockets of their suppliers. They say their main concern is to provide the cheapest sales price to the customer, but it appears the real bottom line is the profits they make for themselves. They all pretend to be America friendly but there doesn't seem to be any loyalty in encouraging "Made in USA" products on their shelves. Maybe what people dislike most about the Big Box stores is that these stores eliminate the small locally owned stores.

Big Box stores hire a lot of clerks but most of the goods they sell are made overseas. Lets remember again what effect that has on America. Those goods coming in from other countries bypass all jobs from the raw goods plants to manufacturing and just skip to our docks on the West Coast and are dispersed out of there to the stores. Sounds simple enough but what is bypassed is the heart of America, the working class American.

Profits from the Big Box stores go to the national headquarters of their chain compared to profits staying locally. There is a reason the family that owns Wal-Mart stores are some of the richest people in the world. America has given them so much; can't they help to give America back its jobs? I prefer not to shop at Wal-Mart but if you do, would you take a minute and write Wal-Mart and ask them to tell their vendors they want products made in the USA,

After all this, do you think Big Box contributes to the job loss in America?

Picture this, you are a vendor that wanted to be competitive so you took your manufacturing overseas in able to sell your products in the Big Box stores. Suddenly the Big Box stores said they would only continue to buy from you if your product was "Made in the USA". If you are a manufacturer you will stop bringing in products from overseas and again have them made in the USA; if you don't you will soon be out of business.

Wal-Mart policies are considered "just good business" and no one is big enough to compete with them but there is one way to get their attention. If you have to shop there stop buying any thing they handle that is not made in the USA what a dramatic event that would be since most of their products are made overseas.

If Big Box stores don't carry what you are looking for with a 'Made in USA' label then go to a local smaller store and see what they have. Even knowing these national chain companies are taking an unfair advantage of the local competition and taking advantage of its suppliers/vendors you might still continue to shop there for the convenience. Maybe your attitude is "who cares, they save me money and no one I know has lost their jobs". That is certainly an honest response and one that is shared with the other shoppers at Big Box stores.

Remember we are looking at all the things that are going on that effect our economic crisis. Whatever changes we can make in each area may pay off in getting things changed. Big Box stores are here to stay, but can't we do something to encourage them to buy American goods?

What Big Box stores need to remember is that the customers that walk through their doors are Americans and if they really care about their customers they will do what they can to give Americans back their jobs.

I understand Wal-Mart is now starting to have goods made in China under their own label. This certainly eliminates the vendor; another part of the food chain Wal-Mart keeps for itself. Wal-Mart now has about 40 stores in China.

Chapter 8

A Plea to Wal-Mart

It is easy to complain about anything going on in our society but any criticism should be followed by a proposal on how to solve the problem. I am throwing in this chapter to show a possible fast way to get things made in the USA.

In the writing of this book, there is one thing that is clearly evident, that neither the US Government nor manufacturers will budge on their belief that the world is a better place because of globalization. The profit margins awaiting companies that take their manufacturing overseas are phenomenal. The US Government allowed this globalization with the encouragement of both big business and foreign countries and they are not about to break the trade agreements they set up.

The American economy can't wait for years to see if we can elect officials that will understand the economic crisis we are in and actually do something about it. America, the greatest country in the entire world, is being brought to its knees and the average American will suffer greatly because of it. We have no place to turn. We thought our best interest was being looked after but we were wrong.

To the Walton family that owns Wal-Mart, I ask you to forgive my forward request but I do not know where else to turn. Your company is the biggest retailer in America and the vendors certainly have to bend to your wishes to be allowed to sell their products in your store. Could you have it in your heart to give your vendors a deadline and after that date Wal-Mart will only accept goods made in the USA? The destruction heading toward America can be avoided by this action. Right now our leaders are doing nothing and I think you can still be listed as some of the richest people in the world if you take this action. This is a great chance to give back to America in a very big way. Give us back our future. You will go from a villain in my eyes to a hero.

As I recall Sam Walton used to pride himself in buying American goods. The average person that shops in Wal-Mart is certainly the working person. There is no greater gift that you could give your customers and give to America than to be the first store to recognize the destruction going on in America and the first to step forward and do something about it.

As noted in this book, I am pleading with Americans to totally stop buying goods that are not made in America. That action could eventually catch on but an action by Wal-Mart would have an immediate effect.

Other countries may become angry but this action is coming from the American people. We just want to get back what the government and manufacturers took away from us. The idea of a global economy was an idealistic theory to support their actions of deserting America.

We don't want America to slip into bankruptcy before someone takes some corrective action. If Wal-Mart would step up and do this, I can guarantee you that there will be a dramatic increase in Wal-Mart shoppers, even myself.

If you wonder how important this is hand out questionnaires in each of your stores that ask the question of your customers "Is it important to you that Wal-Mart sell only Made-in-the USA goods, when at all possible?"

Chapter 9

Keystoning to Gouging

A standard rule of thumb in pricing a product is called "Keystoneing" which means that each company that touches the product doubles its price. An example is if I make a product that costs me $5, I will sell it for $10 directly to a retail outlet, they in turn sell it for $20 and so on. That process appears to be fairly consistent in most manufacturing industries.

When goods are made in the USA everyone knows this pricing structure and most companies can look at your product and pretty well tell what your cost in the product is. The overseas manufacturing is changing all that and Keystoneing is pretty much out the window, here are the reasons.

Goods made in China can be made for as little as 10% to 15% as much as they can be made in the USA. A product made in China for $6 should sell in the USA for $12 plus freight but the trend in this new market concept is to sell it for 10 times more than it cost. They will sell it in the U.S. for $60. They want to sell it for the same amount they used to sell it for in the US but when they made it here it cost them $30 to make it. That difference of $30 to $40 per item doesn't really have a name, some might call it gouging; some might call it just a good business practice. Maybe for the sake of a better word let's call companies that do that "opportunist".

The opportunist shuts down his manufacturing plant in America and immediately reaps the exorbitant profits at the cost of the American economy. If he would pass his savings in making cheap products it would help a lot, but they keep selling them at 'made in the USA' prices. You can see why companies consider it a no-brainer to go overseas. The historic keystoning idea of doubling his price is out the window.

Pick up just about any shoe on the market and you can see evidence of what I'm talking about, buy a pair of Nike, Merrills, or any other brand and pay $100 or more for the shoes that are coming out of the China. The cost to the manufacturer may have only been $10. There is also a new breed of Opportunist that skips the manufacturing and goes directly to places like the TV shopping networks and catalogs. Many of these sellers never did have a manufacturing plant they just went to China and had some goods made and then they go on a show like QVC and start selling them at unbelievable profits. They can sell any product they want as long as they are not infringing on someone else's patents. Most consumer goods are long since past patent protection.

As a Federal Agent I was involved in two different programs that required me to investigate businesses that were charging more than the law allowed. The first program was referred to as the Wage/Price Freeze in the early 1970's. The US Government had frozen all price increases on consumer goods and employee wages and it was my job to determine what companies were not following the rules. We had a lot of violations in all segments of the investigations, the program rolled back prices and wages but it was not a popular program. It was evident that it isn't the government that should be controlling pricing, in a capitalistic economy it should be supply and demand in a free market system.

The next program I was assigned to that tried to control prices was the Federal Energy Program. You may remember the "oil embargo" days of the 1970's. My job was to audit production and pricing of gas and oil from the production wells to the retail pump. We found some violations that required the retailers to reduce their prices at the pump and to refund to the customer's amounts that were overcharged. What I considered to be my most important violation was by a major oil company. When I pursued them I didn't have adequate support from the Federal Energy Administration and I couldn't get the case to court. At that time I discovered how powerful big oil companies are. That was 30 years ago and America is still facing the same gas problems we had back then. All this time no one did anything to try to correct the gas situation.

Maybe the point of the above examples is how tough it is for the US Government to impose regulation on private enterprise. Government intervention is not the American way; it is not the way of capitalism. What has always worked in the past is "let the consumer decide what goes on in the market place". The problem is that the consumer is not organized to protect itself. The corporations are in the position of power and it seems no one is looking after the interest of the average American citizen.

I think most would agree the US Government and big business got us into this mess so let them figure out a way out of it. But here is the problem, neither the US government nor big business thinks there is a problem. It may take another year or two for the US Government to check their tax receipts to discover the tills are running dry. We can't wait for our leaders to look into the problem, because they have their own agenda, they must spend time on pork belly issues, party lines and reelections.

Big business loves the current situation so don't look for them to change anything. They have their hands on a golden goose and they are not about to let go. Profits can magnify to the point their CEO's can draw hundreds of millions of dollars in wages a year and their share holders can still get healthy dividends. But just as important to them is the fact they got to sidestep employee problems, high taxes, union demands, environmental issues and they don't have to repair or replace their factories. Don't expect American companies to let go of these windfall profits.

Chapter 10

Environmentalists/Global Warming

The term "environment" refers to our physical surroundings that affects our lives. Man has always enjoyed his environment, if he didn't he would move to an area that better suited him. In recent years the term of environmentalists is being used to refer to those people who think that no one should be allowed to take any action on public land including mining, logging and oil drilling or take any action that might affect even the smallest of creatures. This very narrow thought process limits placing any economic value on natural resources, beyond just what the naked eye can see. Some people may think that the only ones who truly love the environment should share this sentiment. Many of those people who have this narrow view of the environment were not raised around nature and have viewed it from a distance and walk through 'nature' on weekends while on vacation from the city.

Lets look at another 'environmentalist' with a completely different outlook. A person who has lived their entire life enjoying the scenery of their surroundings, living in the heart of the land some people only see in pictures or while on vacation. They were raised in this environment of timber and mining and hunting, it is all part of their heritage. The love they have for their surroundings is every bit as great as those "city environmentalists" but what really makes them different is the person who was raised in that environment actually understands what makes it all work.

Those people, who live in rural areas, understand the importance of harvesting what nature provides. They love their walks in the woods; they love to see new trees growing where just a few years ago trees were being harvested. Since the woods are part of the economic livelihood of their area they have additional cares and concerns about taking care of these natural resources.

There appears to be a great gap between the two ways of thinking mainly because one side only looks at the scenic value and the others look at the scenic value along with the economic value. Both sides feel that their approach will be better for the future of nature.

Now lets look at what is really happening. Let's see whose approach is winning out.

In the West one of the most heated debates you will hear by its residents is about the impact environmentalists have had on the local economies. Logging is being shut down, lumber mills are closing, mines are being closed down and there is an exodus of people leaving the communities effected. They have to leave to find jobs. The economy they leave behind is in shambles; small businesses as well as those people working in public jobs are being affected. Library staff is cut back as are schoolteachers, and the police departments.

The American system seems to operate a lot on taking action without first looking at the entire problem and what the consequences of their actions are. There is no better example of this than the issue on environment. A true hard core environmentalist wants to close down any development. Period. No more logging, mining, or drilling for oil. That is good in theory isn't it? Keep our back woods area as pristine as they were when they were created.

To hard core environmentalists the economy is not an issue; they could care less what effect it has on the economy. They don't understand that the position they take also does harm to the very woodlands they are trying to preserve.

Lets take a look at the environmental issues about logging and mining. I have worked in both the mining and logging industry so I have had a first hand look at those endeavors. I live in the middle of forest and mining locations and have hunted and hiked these mountains my entire life. If I may, I would like to give you a look at these issues from a first hand prospective.

I now hunt in wooded areas my granddad logged 50 years ago. In my area of the country some of the best hunting is in those areas that have been previously logged. The hunting laws are strict and as a result of good management we have more game now than we did when my grandfather hunted the area.

Trees reach maturity in cold areas slower then they do in the warm climates but still they reach a point where it is best to harvest them and that makes way for a new growth of trees. As a renewable natural resource if it isn't harvested it is wasted, the tree falls over and becomes a fire danger. The 'let burn' tactics of recent years saw millions of acres go up in smoke, they think that is the way nature intended it. There is now an effort being made to stop forest fire fighting because fire fighters have been losing their lives. Where do those people live that think the forest should be just left to burn when there is a fire? A burnt out forest is a very ugly scene for years after the fire.

Most of the fires that get large and out of control are fires that are occurring in areas that have never been logged. The dry downfall trees in those areas cover the ground, rotting and going to waste. In areas that have been previously logged there are roads going into them so firefighters can rapidly get up to the fire areas and the roads themselves can become fire stops. Last summer I delivered supplies to a fire crew in exactly that situation. The fire was contained to just a thousand acres, but had it not been for the roads tens of thousands of acres could have been lost and a small community would have been in harms way.

Letting our forest go 'up in smoke' rather than log them is not good for the animals nor the environment. That action wastes a valuable natural resource. Fires that are let burn destroy everything in their path. Most wild animals can't get out of the fires path so they are all destroyed. The economic value to the logging community is lost. The goods that those logs could have made will never reach market. Letting it burn also increases pollution in the area, which is also a contradiction to wise management.

The evergreen trees in many areas in the western U.S. are now turning brown because they are infested with tree killing insects. Most of the insects doing the damage prefer the mature trees to infest. Had there been proper forest management in these areas there would have been a combination of old and new growth and entire forests would not be now turning brown. The irony of this is that the locations where this is happening are areas where many rich environmentalism have expensive seasonal homes. Their efforts to close down logging are reaping them an eye full of brown trees that will become a gigantic fire hazard. This is what happens when you look at only one side of an issue.

What is the trade off in logging? Environmentalists want to be able to come into the area and take a walk and see no sign that man has been there. They incorrectly think it is best for the wildlife. To those people I say, come on a winter day with fresh snow and we'll walk into areas where there has been logging and you will see a lot of game and wildlife tracks. Then we'll walk into an area that has never been logged and as you crawl over dead falls you will notice the absence of both tracks and animals. Deer and elk will stand and watch you log, they are used to hearing chain saws. They may retreat from close contact but they don't leave the area. Animals still need those areas where they can go into the timber and hide but they don't need the entire forest. To those of you that have never seen an elk they are as big as a horse.

Come and walk through the towns like Libby, Montana where the logging and mills have been shut down after a hundred years of providing jobs for the community and wood products for the rest of the country. See the empty streets and closed businesses and the children having to leave town as soon as they get out of school because the generations of being loggers have came to an end. This same town has also been in the national news because of the damage asbestos mining did to the workers in the area many years ago. Asbestos is a good example of how knowledge changes over years and we have to change our ideas of what we should be doing. I was in asbestos mine back in the 1950's as a kid and played with some of the rock. When you pick it up and rub on it fibers break off and you can see why it turned out to be an unhealthy product. We learn as we go.

Next lets walk down the streets of logging towns in Canada and see what a boom place they are. They are like the towns used to be in America, people working, logging trucks coming down the street heading for the mills. In short, life is good. Does that mean Canadians are smarter than we are? Maybe they realize the economic value of harvesting a renewable resource rather than the "let it burn" philosophy of American environmentalists? They realize that if you want a forest for your kids and grandkids you have to harvest the trees.

Even environmentalists must admit we need lumber goods. The chairs we sit on, the bed we sleep on, the house we live in, even our wooden toothpicks all come from wood. Canada is now providing a lot of our lumber needs, which is okay with environmentalists for two reasons. #1 They don't think it effects them; they still have a job. #2 They have no idea what makes an economy work #3 They are lacking basic knowledge about timber use and what is best for the timber and the animals that live there.

I once read a statement by a wise old man that said; "When you are put in charge of natural resources you had better know how to use them. To preserve something you must use it." Timber is the very best example of this statement. If you don't use it then it goes to waste.

The approach to logging should be to log with as little damage to the land as possible and of course, that is how most loggers work. On private land the landowner wants care taken to prevent erosion after the loggers leave. He wants trees to grow back so the next generation will have something to harvest. The US Forest Service monitors the logging on public lands but they usually have their hands tied by environmentalist's court actions. Just because there are examples of poor logging efforts we shouldn't be shutting down the forest, instead we should be finding ways to improve our logging operations. Each location and logging operation is different but we are all working toward the same end. There is an operation near Missoula, Montana that logs using helicopters to fly the logs out of an area rather than build roads.

One US Forest Service log sale was shut down by a college student from back east who had read about the sale and filed a lawsuit to stop the logging. When he was interviewed he admitted he had never been in the timber and didn't know anything about logging but he just thought he should try to protect the timber. His thought process is exactly what most environmentalists think; to protect the timber we must stop all logging. That individual shut down just one small area timber sale. In the bigger picture during the Clinton/Gore Administration 50 million acres of land owned by the United States Government was closed to logging and oil exploration. The Bush administration is trying to get that action reversed but to date has not succeeded.

Mining is a different game but with the same consequences. You shut down mining and you shut down one of our nations greatest resources. As I mentioned earlier what has made America great are its work force, natural resources and our ability to use them. When you shut down mining you shut down a great source of wealth and you shut down the jobs that go with them. Mining, like logging, makes a long trail of jobs with the end results of usable goods that contribute to our standard of living and our economy.

If environmentalists are concerned about the environment it is good to remember that if the logging or mining is taking place in the US we can have control of the process. If it is being mined or logged out of the country then we have no control. I understand other countries are really polluting the atmosphere and the US can't control it, but we could if we were doing our own milling and refining. The stories go on and on about how badly China is polluting the air and water as they make goods for the US.

Having grown up in a logging/mining area I find it very interesting to see mining test holes here and there when I am out in the woods. Some of them I know my granddad dug. If it had been an actual working mine you would see an old deserted log cabin close by. This is America folks; that old miner's efforts are what developed the west. If the ore leads were strong entire towns grew up like Butte, Montana. If the ore faded fast they became ghost towns like Virginia City.

Had environmentalists been around in those days it is hard to say where we would be now. Granted, there were some environmentally incorrect approaches to mining but no one suggested they be shut down. Today we have very strict laws about how an operation can extract the ore and mill it. That is what we need, good sound practices but don't make them so tough that it shuts down mining. We are getting closer and closer to shutting down all mining and oil exploration in America and that would be a grave mistake.

The attitude of "shut it down and damn the economic results" is being used in all phases of America and it can't go on forever. At the very heart of America is, and always has been, our economy and we should be looking after it like a child we cherish. If we don't look after it then it will die. We need the strong economy to pay for our spending habits, our foreign gifts, our expanded military, our homeland security; none of these things create money. Anything you do to shut down our economy will eventually start cutting into our ability to pay for our extravagances and to provide for our own basic needs.

To environmentalists I say, "do your research". I have lived my research. My friends and family have worked in the mines and in the woods and I know for a fact we love all of nature as much or more than anyone. We want it to be here for their grandchildren. We want to see timber still being harvested, we don't like to see hundreds of thousands of acres of timber that has been blackened by some "let it burn" policy or turning brown because of insects. We know if they log it today our kids and grandkids will log it again in 40 years.

A lot of people in a lot of towns have seen their community destroyed by the stopping of logging and mining. After 3 or 4 generations of providing local jobs and paying taxes and providing valuable products for the rest of our nation this entire process has came to an end.

A few misinformed environmentalists have succeeded in disrupting one of the most important segments of any successful economy, the harvesting of its natural resources and the multiplying effects of the related jobs. But that is okay isn't it? After all we can get our natural resources from overseas and our loggers and miners can find other work. The small towns that were destroyed weren't important, in the big picture it involved a very small percentage of our population.

Is this shutting down of our natural resources an unimportant event, or is it one more nail in Americans coffin? One more way America has lost its independence. One more area we have to depend on other countries for our necessities. One more hole in this bucket we call our economy.

I think the average person knows what we should be doing. Shouldn't we be finding better ways to log and mine to minimize damages to our environment rather then shutting them down? Is something wrong with our system when one person who has never set foot in the woods be allowed to shut down a logging operation? Shouldn't we all spend more time looking at all sides of an issue before we make judgement and definitely before we take legal action to change something we really know nothing about?

At the very heart of America is and always has been our great economy. This great nation depended on our economy and now every day we see people taking action as if the economy is of no importance. Well it is important. Everything that America stands for can be taken away if we continue to make bad choices about our jobs and our environment.

Another area that environmentalists have done grave damage to our economy is in the area of our food resources. We have seen irrigation water taken away from farmers in Oregon because a previously unknown sucker fish was discovered in the river. The farmers and ranchers of our foods, whether it is fruit, vegetables, or cattle are all in the same boat, they are under the control of people who think the providing of America's foods is not important.

As a result of all the obstacles our food producers have to go through to produce our food more and more of them are selling out and turning their land over to developers. Foreign imports are effecting the pricing so much that it is harder for them to make a living producing our vital food goods.

Now we are facing another issue and that is America is becoming dependent on our food source coming in from other countries. Does that sound familiar? Our shoes, shirts, tools, toys, paper, lumber and now our food are coming from other countries. Does that put America in a vulnerable position?

We are just being informed that those fruits and vegetables coming in from other countries are far more contaminated than items produced in the USA. Those other countries don't have the strict production and sanitation requirements that we have so what can we expect.

Environmentalists must understand the economic effect of shutting down our natural resources including items from our food chain. When you live in a country that is so dependent on a strong economy you cannot make environmental decisions without considering the economic impact as part of your equation. If you don't like a particular spray that is used on fruit trees, then become active in trying to find another way to control insects rather than force the closure of the fruit orchard.

The countries that are now starting to produce more and more of our crops may well be contaminating the world far worse than if we were producing our own. The question now being asked is whether or not we really need to have the country of origin placed on our food products. That answer is, of course, yes.

We have become a nation that allows one or two people to file a lawsuit and stop an entire industry. That isn't right. Things like this effect us all and we should all be working toward a middle ground.

We all know we need food, plastics, wood and metals so lets try to find a way to improve the production of these products rather then just shutting down the production of these goods in America and let some other country make our goods for us.

Environmentalists, the way you are now doing business has become another cog in the killing of America. Look into your act and see what you can do to help this great country. Shutting down our mills, our timber production, our crop fields, our mines and our factories is not the way to reach any goal.

Protecting the environment is certainly a goal we must all be reaching for, but trying to preserve our environment by leaving it untouched is detrimental to what we are trying to protect.

UPDATE *March 28, 2005*

In the March 2005 issue of Inc. Magazine the cover reads 'CHINA SHOCK'. One of the topics is that the first clouds of toxic waste have hit the California shore.

Today on the Lou Dobbs TV show he showed film from Beijing, China. The view of pollution was beyond anything the world has ever seen. The ingredients of the polluted air included mercury. The people walking down the street were shown covering their faces to keep from breathing the polluted air. The report stated that this air is now beginning to travel around the world. China is the biggest source of pollution in world history. The reason for this is that China is now doing most of the manufacturing for the U.S. and also other countries are starting to follow suit and have their manufacturing done in China.

I knew this would happen but it has taken place far quicker then I would have imagined. This makes it even more important that we have to have an EXIT PLAN to take our manufacturing back from China.

We are being told to cut down on our fish intake due to the increased amount of mercury being found in fish. China pollution is harming the ocean as much as the air. We can do our part to shut down China manufacturing. America is the main culprit that created this problem by giving them all our manufacturing so we have to be a leader in solving it.

UPDATE: *2007*

When I first wrote this book I hadn't heard much about global warming and now it is a major issue. I saw the Al Gore movie AN INCONVENT TRUTH showing how bad global warming has become.

Mr. Gore may not remember that when he was in office as Vice President his environmental actions are what helped close our factories and forests. The Clinton/Gore team stopped logging on public land and created many of the problems I talk about in this book. Al Gore was in the middle of this entire program but his actions went deeper than the just the environment. He may have been taking funds for his reelections from those countries (mainly China) that are polluting the world. I see Gore is still in the hunt to be the president of the US, does that sound like a good idea?

UPDATE: March 2007

Dogs and cats around America are dying from something in canned pet foods. It has just been discovered that the ingredients that were poisonous were products that had been imported from China that had a combination of fertilizer and plastic processing compounds. There are now concerns that similar contaminates may have also entered the human food products imported into America from other countries.

Chapter 11

What We Gave Up

When it was decided to give away US manufacturing how much thought was put into understanding what we were giving away. Most manufacturers used to keep a tight lid on what they were making and how they made it. They have worked hard to develop a product and they usually don't want to give it up to the competition. They don't seem to view foreign countries as competition but they are the fiercest of competition and we will soon find that out.

In America's case we have spent 200 years developing our industrial capabilities. We have invented most of the products now on the market. We used hard-earned money from our capitalistic system to design and develop our entire system from the ground up. Our machinery, our products, our history is what made America the most important manufacturing nation in the world. Our great grandparents, down to our parents and ourselves developed every thing we had.

We brought our manufacturing to a level unmatched in the world and we did that while improving human rights, health and welfare. The countries we gave our manufacturing to don't have that same respect for human life. Our system rewards those who stick out their necks to develop new and improved things. Our system created a wealth that allowed us to have a strong government with a strong military. Our wealth allowed us to have a military that over the years has been called upon to help protect other ideals and other countries in the free world.

Did the countries that we have given our manufacturing to do anything to deserve the right to take all this from us? While we were struggling to perfect this great manufacturing system many of those nations stuck by their communist agenda.

We have cloned China into what is now the biggest manufacturing country in the world. We have always bought things from China, silks and China dishes; China has historically given us some of the "nice" things in life. But now China is providing us with our necessities. China has mile after mile of new manufacturing plants while our plants are becoming outdated and are closing down. Many of those new plants in China are powered by coal; one of the worst sources of energy due to the pollution it causes.

Neither China nor most of the other countries we handed our jobs to were involved in the work to create a manufacturing giant. Our ancestors would be shocked to know that after all the work they put in to in creating our economic system it would to be given away to nations half way around the world. When you look at the world globe at the locations that now do our manufacturing and computer work you can see it is all in the area around China and India. We may not know for a few years what that significance is.

We have to ask ourselves, why we did this? Why would a country as smart as the USA simple hand over all its technology and manufacturing abilities to other countries? Is there some hidden agenda we don't know about?

Will our leaders ever get to the point they admit they made a mistake? We know our business leaders are happy with going this way but what about our government leaders that were hired to protect the USA. Did they do it out of stupidity? Out of greed? Were there payoffs being made under the table by foreign countries or by big business?

What we gave away is easy to answer; we gave away everything that our country and our capitalistic system has worked two hundred years to develop. Walk down the streets of Skowhegan, Maine or Libby, Montana and a thousand town's in-between and the empty streets and mills will let you know what we gave away.

What about all the taxes at all levels from city to county to state and federal government? Where will the funds come to operate the government machine that our system had created? Maybe our government has lost sight of where their paychecks come from, but we, the workers haven't lost sight of anything, anything that is except our jobs.

The trend in the US is to think our best and brightest people will become highly educated and their jobs will only involve computers so blue collar jobs are out. Blue-collar workers then become dispensable. People with those thoughts didn't realize that for our existence the blue-collar worker is the most important worker we have. They provide us with every thing we touch. Our manufacturers provide us with paper, chairs, computers, tables, cloths, toys and cars. You name it if you can touch it then it was made by a blue-collar worker.

Computers certainly helped us cut down on the paper chase but let us see what computers will give us to replace what the blue-collar worker used to give us. Remember the concept of "value added"? At every step the blue-collar worker added value to consumer products. The people that made the decision to give away our manufacturing didn't understand the "value added" concept. They didn't know that manufacturing is the foundation of a strong economy.

What we have given up is the very heart of the American economy. Do we have the right to fight to get our jobs back? We not only have the right we have the obligation. This generation of Americans was handed this great country and we are obligated to pass this on to the next generation. We don't want to pass on a country that has to buy all its goods from

Communist China. We are selling our future to another country. I shouldn't say selling our future we are giving it away. It won't be long before we hear the words "Grandpa what happened to America?" Do we want the children in China to have the inheritance that was meant to be for our children?

Chapter 12

Change the System

We have seen our government grow to astronomical proportions and yet they are making many major misjudgments. The idea of public servant has long been discarded and the government has taken on a role all to itself. It seems to make a lot of decisions without regard to how it helps or hinders the average American citizen.

Our leaders have a history of providing pork for pet causes, which usually involved some special project in their own state. In my state we have several new federal buildings named after existing national leaders. We see how many trips our congressman make to foreign countries and how much money they give foreign countries.

Their spending rivals the spending of even the most flamboyant king. They spend like there is no end to the money roll. Now that those very same people have opted to give away our manufacturing jobs they do not seem to understand the American billfold can no longer support their excesses.

How can we change this system and get back to having elected officials at the national level that actually put the citizens of America before any other deals they attempt to make? Wouldn't that be great, the citizens would come before the special interest groups and businesses that donate big money to their re-election campaigns and before any foreign leader they are trying to impress.

It is certainly evident that our leaders have not been looking out for America so something has to change. They don't seem to get the drift yet; the giving away of our jobs is emptying our pockets and has America on a downward spiral that won't end until we get our manufacturing back.

We have to start treating our elected officials like all other government employees. They have to be accountable and they can't take a penny from any source. Now they are only held accountable on Election Day and even then we don't hold them accountable. They are a monster all by themselves, handing out money, spending money, taking bribes and payoffs and being treated like kings with one of the best retirement systems in our country. America is getting so close to being broke that it is amazing. Our leaders have allowed all our jobs to go away and they don't seem to understand how that devastated our tax base. They have spent decades giving billions of dollars away to countries that often turn out to be our enemy. Any vote our elected officials make should meet one basic rule "let us do what is best for America".

Chapter 13

Greed and Power

The dictionary has a very simple definition of greed, "excessive desire for acquiring more than one needs or deserves". If there is anything that drives the world today, especially in America, it is greed. That is a very short explanation for something that has ruined so many lives.

I heard the phrase once that went, "the problem with the rich is that they never have enough". Why do you suppose that is, why can't they ever get enough? Here are some of my thoughts on the subject.

I was raised in a very poor situation. We lived in an old house out in the country that didn't have running water. We hauled water in from the creek. Our only heat was a central wood stove that never seemed to get the heat to the upstairs bedroom where I slept. My parents, especially my mother was the most sharing, caring person I have ever met. She would invite strangers in for supper, give her last nickel to anyone who needed it and would never drive past a stranded motorist. She would do all this without even expecting a thank you.

When you are raised in an environment like this there is no room for being selfish. The idea of having more money, or more of anything, only brought more ideas of how you could share what you have. The idea of getting more and just keeping it for ourselves never entered our minds.

I have a thousand stories of people I have helped in my life but there is one that stands out in my mind as an especially heartfelt happening. My wife and I stopped at a truck stop somewhere in South Dakota and I noticed an old car parked off to the side with a woman and two girls in it. You could tell without asking they were stranded. After I filled up my car I walked over and talked to them. They had spent the night in the car and were trying to figure out how they could get enough money for gas to make it a few hundred more miles to home. I filled up their gas tank and gave them $40 and of course they were elated. She asked for my name and address so she could return the money to me but I told her that wasn't necessary. The woman expressed her amazement that I was so generous but she understood where I was coming from when I told her simply "I've been there."

Maybe more than any other explanation for greed is that phrase "I've been there". What is the background of a greedy person? Maybe more often than not they have never been down and out and know the feeling when someone reached out to help them. They have only experienced the feeling of acquiring for themselves. I know personally the feeling of acquisition, is nothing compared to the feeling I get inside when I help someone in need. It is still all too real to me when I think back on my childhood and remember the people who helped us for no other motive than to help someone in need.

A recent study stated that the most generous people in America are the working poor. They have not only "been there"; they are still there. I have heard rich people say "people are poor because they are too lazy to work". That may apply to a few but certainly not the working poor. I know a lot of poor people and none of them are lazy, they are all hard working people that would share what they have. Each one of them has a story that they don't dwell on, about why they have not acquired much in this life.

Giving is something we can do without fanfare, no one taking pictures of our good deeds, no hanging around expecting a big thank you, no leaving your name and address so they can send your money back. Just do it for yourself, it is a good feeling.

Corporate greed is just a continuation of the same concept. When you are a corporate president you get a wage that compensates you. The shareholders expect you to do a good job for that wage. Up until a few years ago a good wage for a big company executive might be as high as a million dollars a year. For that the shareholders expected loyalty, honesty, integrity and a good return on their investment.

With globalization, corporate leaders found that they could ship a lot of the company work overseas and make a very large amount of money for the company. Soon it became evident that they could take hundreds of millions of dollars in annual salary for themselves and still show a large profit for the company. The shareholders didn't care because they were still making a good return on their investment.

The greedy executive soon discovered that in addition to all the wages and bonuses he could take out of the company he could also go on big spending sprees, partying around the world at company expense. No matter how much he takes out of the company he suddenly wants more and he thinks he deserves it because it was his decision to ship all the jobs overseas. You and I can sit back and view his actions as greedy, but he will go to his grave thinking he deserves it all because after all it was his decision to send the jobs overseas and greatly improve the companies profits. He doesn't give a thought to what his former employee's will have to endure when they lose their jobs.

I just read about the SAS Shoe Company and the Christmas bonus they gave their employees. This is a shoe company still operating in America. The ugly bug called greed must not have bitten their top officers. They haven't sent their manufacturing overseas and they still want to share their success with their workers. I have worn SAS shoes for years; they are the most comfortable shoes on the market. They believe in doing business right, keep manufacturing in the USA and make a top quality product. Thank you SAS for making a great shoe and doing what's right. Nike could still be like that.

Right now in the USA greed and top end profit seems to be the controlling factor. Greed is going to bankrupt this great country. We are like the person who starves himself to death without knowing there is a problem. Our diet of overseas goods has to come to an end because we have fed on that diet so long that it is beginning to eat the muscles of our body, this body called America.

What makes a greedy person so terrible is that his actions can affect hundreds and thousands of people. If you get enough greedy people acting at the same time they can damage an entire nation which is what we have happening in the USA right now. Greedy people are like terrorists; they strike the unsuspecting and those who can't protect themselves. A greedy person can destroy the lives of thousands of men, women and children by just one act of greediness. A greedy corporate executive can bankrupt a company. In my state we have had several companies go under while the top people made off with millions, but the working class people that invested in the company saw their life savings go up in smoke. Many of these people who lost out were retirement age and have no chance to rebuild their nest egg. Many of them have been forced back to work, but as you know when you are 60 or 70 years old it is hard to find jobs.

In the cases I am aware of locally no corporate executive has ever spent a day in jail and have never had to repay the excessive salaries they received. An investor in one of the companies that went under talked to the FBI about the situation and was told that it isn't a crime to pay excessive wages and it was up to the shareholders themselves to draw the line on wages. If you own stock in a company you should contact the company and get the facts about what kind of wages the top executives are drawing and also what kind of bonuses and other benefits they are receiving.

Greedy people don't call themselves greedy, they think of themselves as shrewd, intelligent, taking advantage of situations, and worthy of their take irregardless of its consequences to others.

America has probably the greatest concentration of greedy people in the world. Greed has crept into the decision making of manufacturers and our elected officials. We can do our part by voting out leaders that appear to have been caught up with greed. We can stop buying products from companies that have been caught up with so much greed they take their manufacturing overseas.

Power seems to have the same intoxication to some people as greed. It has been said "You can elect a good man to office but shortly after he arrives in Washington he becomes aware of his sudden power and starts acting accordingly". I don't think people with true wisdom would react that way but Americans seldom seem to elect people with wisdom. When you watch our elected officials speaking on TV they come across as shallow, conceited, one trick pony's with their own agenda. They seem to speak without thinking and they seem to think that the only view that is important is their own, but what bothers me most is they quickly forget they were elected to look out for the welfare of America, not just a few people, but America.

We need officials in office that truly know the significance of their position and don't react to their job as if they are powerful but approach the job as a humble public servant caring for their masters welfare. We all know people like that, doing big things but not making a big deal out of it. Those people seldom run for office.

I recently listened to Henry Kissinger when he was asked whether or not we should have dialogue with Iran. (Remember Bush and Rice have been turning down opportunities to talk to

Iran for years). Mr. Kissinger replied "We should never turn down any opportunity to have dialogue with anyone". Mr. Kissinger won the Noble Prize in 1973 for negotiating a cease-fire between the North and South Vietnamese. Now that is a statesman. As far as I know we have no elected officials currently in office that are in the class of Mr. Kissinger. When he was active in our politics he always just quietly went about doing his job, I don't recall ever seeing him showboating or making comments that weren't well thought out. He accepted power graciously.

Mr. Kissinger was born in Furth, Germany and his calm thought process reflects his European background.

Chapter 14

What Can We Do as Citizens

This book covers a lot of criticism of our corporate and government leaders and it seems only fair that some comments be made to each of us as citizens of this great land. Our founding fathers did what they could to design a system that allowed for a lot of individual rights while still coming together form a strong nation.

We are called a democratic republic for a reason; we get to decide who we want to lead us. We vote for officials and hope they do what is best for our nation as a whole. Decisions have been made in recent years that have literally brought America to its knees financially. We have found that in our attempt to put the blame onto someone, that both the government and the corporate world are a slippery bunch. No one steps up when things go wrong, they make decisions and disappear into the woodwork, people rarely lose their job with the government.

Our President makes a lot of his decisions based on the advice of those aides close to him. He hires or appoints people who are considered experts. Isn't there some way we can have more input into who is hired as presidential advisors? Those aides help make powerful decisions.

We know enough from past experience that the US Government is bigger than an African elephant and is impossible to turn. Some of the public officials that created this monster may have already left office, but a new crew always replaces them with the same mental attitude about ignoring what is best for America as a whole. They have trouble understanding reality economics and globalization. I really don't think the US Government will ever have a hearing on whether or not they should do something about the economics consequences of their actions. Most of them had received contributions from big business, foreign countries, lobbyists and special interest groups so after a few years of debate and haggling no action will be taken.

The corporate world is making so much money; they won't turn their boat around for anything. Their response will be "are you kidding look at this bottom line, the company is making hundreds of millions more by having the work done overseas. Besides everyone else goes overseas and we have to keep doing it to be competitive".

There is no way you will convince the government or the companies to stop going abroad with our jobs. That is pretty depressing isn't it? President Clinton with his vision of globalization has signed a deal to bankrupt America and the US won't back down on its word.

What can we do as citizens? Stop buying goods made out of country. Stop dealing with companies that have outsourced their computer and telephone functions to India. That is a big order isn't it? Our government is organized, big corporations are organized and they both seem to be able to do anything they want.

So why can't American citizens individually organize into a 290 million strong mob, and say, "no more, we will no longer buy anything that is made overseas"? That sounds like something we can do. Just remember that on every shopping trip you make, every day of the week. No more foreign goods. We could make a difference.

We must learn to spend wisely and elect wisely.

Chapter 15

Who Were Those Guys

In the 1990's President Clinton was given credit as the person that brought about globalization. When he was in office he spent a lot of time going around the world talking to all the countries that ended up taking our jobs. What a beautiful way to spread the ideas of capitalism and help 3rd world countries. Let them do our manufacturing.

As we now look at the devastation those actions are causing the United States it certainly seems like a good time to ask the question "Who were those guys?" Who were the people that sat down with President Clinton and concocted this plan to actively open countries up so they can make the goods Americans were making for ourselves?

By now we all know the consequences of that decision but I still wonder about who the people were that met with Clinton to arrive at a decision with such a magnitude? One would suppose that they were all highly educated advisors since Clinton did surround himself with his friends with MBA's PhD's, and law degrees. But who were they beyond that. Did any of those people have any actual experience doing anything? Did any of them ever run a manufacturing business? Did any of them have even a friend or relative that worked at a blue-collar job? Clinton spent his life working for the government so we know he had no experience with real world economics. It would be interesting to know just where they were coming from.

Was there anyone present that had received any donations from big business? How many businesses came bearing gifts of money to the Clinton/Gore reelection campaign? If the accusations are true about Clinton getting money from foreign countries then those countries were better represented than the American people were at those meetings.

We don't know who was there in person or via a silent proxy but we are pretty sure we know who wasn't in on the meetings. Those absent were representatives of the textile workers, garment workers, toy and tool workers, loggers or miners or any of the supporting companies that supplied goods and services to those workers. Was any union represented at those meetings? Was there anyone present that had actually ever worked manually for a living?

Since this meeting was to have such a dramatic effect on every person in America I would hope the average citizen was properly represented. We had at least one elected official in the form of President Clinton but he takes credit as being the mastermind behind it so we know how he voted. But who were the others present for the planning of this great event that is quickly becoming the most expensive action ever taken against the USA. It is costing Americans more than all the wars, floods, hurricanes and fires combined so who else was involved? Can we point to some of Clinton's well-educated advisors or just leave all the blame on Clinton?

Chapter 16

Stock Market

Most economists point to the strong stock market to reassure us that the American economy is doing great. The companies that have had their stocks staying strong are those that sent their jobs overseas. Every time a company announces they are closing their US facilities their stock goes up. To me that isn't a sign that the economy is doing strong, it only means that the shareholders in that company can now expect a better stock dividend from that company.

The stock market will take a dive when it is found that America is in trouble as a result of the side effects of sending our jobs overseas.

When Americans demand goods again be made in the USA it will have a dramatic effect on the stock market. The companies will have to spend a lot of their profits building factories here in the US. The adjustments that will come in stock prices will be abrupt but in the long run this entire scenario will be part of the saving of America.

Chapter 17

Bill Clinton

I have already talked a lot about Clinton, but he did so much damage to America he deserves his own chapter. In the early 1990's stories were starting to surface that Clinton was taking money from both Korea and China. Reports said that a half dozen foreign businessmen gave large amounts to the Clinton/Gore reelection funds but it was suspected that those funds actually originated from the countries involved.

As the stories surfaced the general population seemed to discount the thought that there was any importance to those happenings even though they were actually against the law. Clinton said in a news conference that he "was appalled when he first learned his campaign had taken illegal foreign donations in 1996" (statement made on 3-29-2000). Instead of developing into another Clinton scandal the entire thing just disappeared. Some said at that time, there were so many public officials taking illegal money that none of our elected officials wanted to pursue the situation.

What Clinton did was the same thing Thomas Friedman did in writing THE WORLD IS FLAT and LEXUS AND THE OLIVE TREE. They both went around the world talking to many countries about how it would help that country to become part of the manufacturing process of the world. The real problem came in when they apparently didn't tell those countries that to become part of this great globalization movement they should create their own markets and manufacturing. I wasn't at those meeting but it would appear that they suggested to those countries like China and India that the American manufacturing was available for them to take over. Somewhere along the line it must have been implied that Americans no longer needed those manufacturing jobs.

Like Mr. Friedman, Clinton never gave a thought to the economic consequences that action would have on America. Neither of these people have a working knowledge of basic economic concepts like "jobs creates jobs" and the multiplying effect of the entire process of producing our own goods. They didn't know the importance of America being self-sufficient. They didn't seem to understand the gigantic effect the sending away of jobs would have on America's entire tax system. The writings of Mr. Friedman capture the picture of how our leaders thought in the 1990's and early 2000's. Those best selling books will remain as a blue print of how stupid and arrogant the America leaders had become, a blue print of what goes wrong when we ignore basic economics. Mr. Clinton's lack of knowledge took America from being a self-sufficient country to a country dependent on the rest of the world for most of its manufactured goods.

When we look back on it, the opening up of the trade corridors with China, was the most important single event in US history. That event has cost the USA millions of jobs and billions of dollars and it is only starting. If allowed to continue at its current pace, it has the ability to cripple the US economy while at the same time it will make China the most powerful country in the world, thanks to US dollars pouring in. When Clinton handed our manufacturing over to China he must have forgotten America had been fighting Communism for 50 years. Based on how things turned out we have to now go back and look at the millions of dollars the Clinton/Gore team brought into their reelection funds from those countries. It is no longer a simple question of campaign ethics, it becomes an issue of selling out America. Treason might be too strong of a word but their actions were very close to that.

We were caught off guard.

We are now honoring trade agreements with China that appears to have been negotiated under illegal conditions. That country may have bought the United States President in a way that was illegal under US campaign-financing laws. An investigation should be immediately conducted. If it is found that the Clinton/Gore campaign funds contained money that can be traced back to foreign governments through foreign companies, the countries involved should lose their trade status or renegotiate with more controls. We know many of our other elected officials, like John Kerry also got reelection funds from foreign sources. I wonder how many people are still in office that received those funds? Maybe every elected and appointed official at that time had fund raising skeletons in their closets.

At the time of the allegations, Attorney General Reno had a staff of investigators on the case. At this time those investigations should be considered invalid. It doesn't appear that anyone in Washington DC wanted campaign finances disclosed.

The importance of the Clinton/Gore actions makes it necessary to look again at their tactics. It is imperative for many reasons, including seeing if we are in trade agreements based on illegal activities and also it puts our elected officials on notice that the American people will no longer tolerate the selling of our elected officials.

This investigation must be conducted by a group of people unrelated and unattached to the Washington system or any party alliance. I believe the most reliable investigators would be retired IRS and FBI agents. Take a dozen of these agents and give them unlimited access to the Clinton/Gore campaign funds for the years 1994 through 2000 and I guarantee they will find the truth. In charge of that group could be retired supervisors, one each from the IRS and FBI.

No elected or currently employed public servant should have anything to do with the investigations or the findings. When the investigation is completed, the findings would be aired directly to the public. Everyone seems to like reality TV, that is the quickest way to get information passed to the public. This "cut to the chase" approach will put our elected officials and our public employees on notice that the people of the US are tired of scams and having our country given away, or in this case sold. It will put the world on notice that the days of trying to bribe US officials are over.

America has been betrayed by these events that gave (or sold) our jobs and our future. The situation is worsening by the minute. Every day more companies in the US are closing their doors so they can go overseas to make our products.

I don't know about you, but it makes me mad. As far as Clinton is concerned I wish we could strip him of the millions of dollars of benefits we still have to pay him, but that might be unrealistic. One thing we can do is never let him back into any position in our government. To me that also means not letting him in the back door by electing his wife Hillary as our next President. Many say that Hillary was the real brain behind Clinton's decisions.

The Clinton/Gore team came in with their agenda of "globalization" and completely ignored the cause and effects of their decisions to send our manufacturing overseas. They closed our natural resource harvesting and closed our factories in the name of caring for the environment. In spite of all the damage done by this team, a lot of Americans still like Bill Clinton, they don't care how much damage he did to America. From my point of view I consider his actions to be the most destructive in American history.

Chapter 18

Entertainment

A country that is strong and wealthy can support the arts and any form of entertainment that it wants. The Roman Empire was certainly noted for their entertainment and also for their quest to conquer the world and they were apparently a very wealthy nation for its time. There is no doubt the Romans were so rich and powerful that they thought they could keep on going to war and spending money on entertainment forever. As we now know that was not the case.

What the Romans may not have been aware of is that both wars and entertainment have to be paid for by the working class. Somebody has to be making the consumer goods and making profits that will create enough excess that you can pay for armies and still have enough left over to indulge in entertainment. In Rome the upper class took their eyes off of their workers and forgot what it takes to make a strong stable country. Their eyes went around the world while at home they just wanted to be entertained. Maybe the Romans also thought they were above needing the working class.

In America we have the greatest realm of entertainment ever know to man and that is because we have been one of the richest nations to ever exist. We have movies, sports, TV's, video games, and computers and even hunting has become a big sport.

We are quickly becoming a nation that spends more of its time and money on our entertainment than we do on anything else. We pay our sports and entertainment people hundreds of millions of dollars to keep us entertained. We also use entertainment to baby sit our children.

Now that our economy is suffering we are finding that even our entertainment is going to suffer. More and more people are finding it hard to provide their own basics of life. Every day more Americans are becoming homeless, filing for bankruptcy and just struggling to survive.

Gambling has become big entertainment throughout the country. It will take as much money as you throw at it. We are not only using it for entertainment but now as our economy worsens people are gambling more to try and pick up extra money.

A friend of mine is one of the best artists in the country, making quality western bronzes. In the last couple years he has seen the sales of his art declining dramatically because even the middle and upper class people are starting to feel the crunch of the economy. Higher paid corporate office workers are finding their jobs being outsourced to India. Everyone has friends or relatives losing their jobs at all levels so things like pieces of art and entertainment have fallen from their shopping list.

The point I am trying to make is that our government officials and corporations have given away more than just jobs. They have put our very way of life in jeopardy, at every level from entertainment to education, and put in jeopardy the very future of our children.

Chapter 19

Polls—What Does America Want

Every day on the news we see polls that tell us what we are thinking. They tell us that the average American thinks the economy is recovering and that we are still very satisfied with our leaders. Polls tell us that the unemployment rate is down. Most of the polls make it sound like everything is okay in America.

I seldom hear poll results that reflect what my friends and I are thinking. I wonder whom they are polling? Do they have groups of people they call that live in an area far from reality? Certainly any question you ask a person will have an answer that is a direct response to his life style. Ask a man who has no trouble paying his bills what he thinks of the economy and he will say it is great. That same man will also say he likes the way the government is operating.

Ask a person in a depressed area, say in a logging town where the timber industry has been shut down by actions taken by the government to appease environmentalists, and he will have a story of gloom and doom. He will be a man that can't pay for the basics in life for his family and is now looking for work.

There was a poll recently that had a conclusion that my friends and I would agree with. In that poll they asked what direction America should be taking. The answer was very simply "We just want to be left alone." I think that statement is the poll that is the most important one for our leaders to understand. We just want to be left alone. Of course that is now almost impossible, but it is something we can strive for.

What would it take for Americans to get their wish of just being left alone? Couldn't we (individually and our government) start demanding our manufacturing be brought back home? Couldn't our government go back to the days when we wanted to be a strong country without trying to force the world to our way of thinking? These are the types of things that America really wants.

Maybe what America wants most of all is to be able to elect officials that have honesty and integrity and would never accept a penny from anyone for any reason? Those people would go to Washington and spend their elected years doing what is best for America. They would not base their decisions on the desires of some small group who slipped them money for reelection.

As Americans we shouldn't have to worry about other countries slipping our leaders money under the table to sway how they vote on an issue. No one has the right to hand our public officials money for any reason. They are being paid by the taxpayer and we are tired of under the table bribes being given to our employees. And we want to tell our officials to leave other countries alone, quit imposing our will around the world.

The elected officials already in office will not sit by quietly while America tries to impose such a system. The soft money is part of their gravy train so this will be a tough system to break. The new people who are trying to get elected should be made to publicly, and in writing, agree to not accept a penny from any source. Prior to elections we can ask those already in office to agree to this "no money from outsiders" provision and if they don't agree make their decision known to the voters. Americans just want to be left alone and we want our elected officials to be left alone. We are in a life and death fight for our country and things have to change.

Americans understand that the price of making China the biggest manufacturer in the world came out of our pocket. We will now watch as they become the biggest and most powerful country in the world at the expense of the US. We watch as our tax base shrinks both relating to income taxes and social security taxes. China in the mean time grows stronger by the minute on our dollar. Their economy and their military are about to blow by the US.

Most Americans polled would say, "ENOUGH IS ENOUGH."

Chapter 20

Education

Americans believe in education. We would like to see every person have, at least, a high school education. Education would enable people to conduct most of their own affairs since they will be able to read write and do math.

In recent years some Americans have come to believe that a college education is necessary to find success and a Masters or Ph.D. is even better. Success is determined by the degree you hold, at least that is how some people think but in reality that is not the case. Education certainly helps us get to the level we want to be in our society, but it is only one tool that must be blended with a good work ethic and work experience.

A person who has a high school diploma who started his own business from scratch and ended up 6 years later with a successful business is far more educated in economics than the person with a Ph.D. in economics. In our society, we will hire the person with the degree to teach our students about economics and will even buy the books the man with the Ph.D. in economics writes but that does not necessarily mean he understands cause and effect reality economics. This is starting to become a very real problem in the USA.

People with the degrees are also becoming the advisors that the government looks to when they are considering economic policy. That situation occurred with Clinton when a few of his highly educated advisors came up with the idea of globalization. Clinton said in one interview that we will become a country that exports technology and he traded our manufacturing jobs for the theory that Americans will find jobs in the computer and technology areas. It is too bad that he hadn't looked for advice from people who had experience in real life economics instead of with people with high degrees. Experience brings reality to the table, education brings theory. This has never been better shown than this entire fiasco of allowing our manufacturing to be sent out of the USA.

In fields of exact science, degrees are necessary to get onto the playing field. Degrees in physics, medicines, and anything to do with research and science require you to have a degree to speak the language. If you don't know math and science you can't get in the door. To be a medical doctor, in addition to a degree, you have to be an intern for 3 years, to see if you can actually apply the things you learned. They want you to not only read about doing surgery they want you to have hands on experience under the guidance of one with experience.

Unfortunately in business and economics that requirement of actual experience does not exist. You can get your Ph.D. and then go right into teaching, advising the government or writing a book without a minute of hands on experience. You are then considered an expert and yet you have no experience.

Just before I graduated from college I was sitting on campus in the four-story school library feeling good that I was about to become the first person in my family to get a college degree. I am not sure if I was feeling smart or if I was just reflecting on my accomplishment, I know I didn't feel like I knew it all. A woman went by with a cart full of books replacing them on the shelves. When I saw that, I wondered just how many books I had read in my 4 years of college. Did I read enough to fill up 3 or 4 carts? Maybe I read 100 books total to get my degree. Then I wondered how many books were in that library, no doubt at least a few hundred thousand books. That certainly was a reminder to me how little I knew even with a college degree.

One time a friend asked me which I thought was more important, the 3 years I spent in the Army or the 4 years I spent in college. I could answer that question without hesitation. The 3 years in the Army taught me so much more than college did. The Army had taught me about life, I had to leave the self-centered person I was behind. I was taught to never miss a meeting, to be willing to work 20-hour days if needed. It taught me that every decision you make has consequences that affect others and it is you that have to pay for any mistakes you make. Maybe, most importantly, it taught me that my individual wants and needs were always less important then the needs of my unit or the Army. The Army taught me to have a lot of love and respect for my country. My love for my country was really enhanced when I was sent overseas, from the time I was 18 years old until I was 21. The phrase "On our watch" is a military term meaning you are responsible for everything that happens when you are in charge. Owning my own business taught me about the economic consequences of every decision we make. My 4 years of college and 27 years as a government investigator taught me how to dig for the truth.

In summary, education is one of our most important tools when it is mixed with experience. I have met many educated people who give you a sense that their degrees make them superior. What is ironic about their feelings of self-importance is that any man who owns a business can spot one of those "economic theorists" a mile off. Bottom line, a degree in business or economics only means you have a degree "in theory" and that degree should show the theory aspect, such as Ph.D. in Economic Theory.

A few years ago I attended a college graduation and noticed something that may become a concern for Americans. The higher degrees in science and math seemed to be awarded to foreign students, especially Asian. Is this a trend?

Chapter 21

Our Inheritance

Can you imagine how hard Americans worked a hundred years ago to make us the manufacturing capital of the world? Picture your great grandfather working hard in a factory in 1907 and someone walking up to him telling him in 100 years America is going to give all our manufacturing to China, for nothing, not a dime, except what the Clinton/Gore team received.

For 200 years America looked after itself and tried to be a silent friend to other nations. We were an example of a democratic nation; we worked hard and reaped the rewards. We were never an aggressive nation trying to impose ourselves on other countries. In the last 40 years that attitude has changed, now we think we can control the world with our military might. We want everyone to be a democracy but we are doing it in a very unusual manner. We are giving away our jobs, manufacturing and money to countries like Communist China whom we all know may be one of the worst offenders of human rights in the world.

Think of America as a ship that we started building 200 years ago. The bottom of the ship was our natural resources, which we turned into the 2nd layer of the ship, which was manufacturing. As we got richer we started hiring public servants to look after our interests. The third layer of the ship then became the US Government. As we got richer we added even a 4th layer of US Government workers. With each layer we thought we were getting our moneys worth, after all they were hired and paid for by America. It made no difference to us if the workers were elected, appointed, or hired off the street they all had the same assignment. That assignment was to look after what's best for America.

When a country is developing, it gets more and more involved in the finer things of life. It adds the arts, entertainment and sports and this becomes the 5th tier of the boat. Now a lot of people want to come to America so we add another deck for the immigrants, which is our 6th deck.

This gigantic boat called America is certainly storm worthy and is guaranteed not to sink. There is room for us all to live productive lives. When the system is working right, this boat sails like none other, most people are working and with this prosperity, we can enjoy the fruits of our labors.

But now comes a problem. The 3rd and 4th layer called the government decide that America no longer needs the 1st tier of the boat called natural resources nor do they need the 2nd tier called manufacturing. After making this decision our government closes down our natural resource development and allows other countries to take over our manufacturing.

The Clinton/Gore administration ignored the fact that our natural resources and manufacturing are what made America rich. I am not sure where they thought the money came from to run our government. I think they thought we only needed office jobs to survive.

This great country of America, that our wise and ambitious forefathers built, is suddenly put in jeopardy by just one generation. The generation of people born after 1945 does not remember the struggles our country went through to get to this point. We were born into an affluent economy that would last forever, so why worry. We elected people to head our government that didn't seem to have a clue where money comes from. Our leaders were sending hundreds of millions of our dollars to other countries where most of it landed in the personal accounts of the foreign leaders.

America is no longer an unsinkable ship. Our leaders have given away the most important part of our economic system. How do they expect us to afford the layers of government workers we now have? How do they expect us to still be able to spend so much on arts, sports, and entertainment when our workers have lost their jobs?

The Titanic was unsinkable until its lower levels sprung a leak. That is the situation the USA is now in. Our leak is the disappearance of our jobs, both in the factory and now with outsourcing in our offices. Our natural resources were almost shut down under the Clinton/Gore reign. Can we repair the gigantic hole the Clinton days allowed? Sure we can if we can convince our leaders that America has had enough, The Titanic was sunk by an outside source, an iceberg, when the skipper ignored the potential danger because he thought the boat was unsinkable. The hole in America's ship was created by people who didn't seem to have a clue what they were doing and ignored all the warnings.

ENOUGH IS ENOUGH. We want our country back. We want what we inherited. A country that could provide for itself. A country that places its own people above all others. Let us go back to the concept of what is important, a country that proudly produces its own consumer products, and a country that looks after it's own people first.

Elected officials, greedy corporations, economists and environmentalists have stolen our inheritance and America wants it back. If they don't give it back we want them replaced. Corporations that won't manufacture goods in the USA, you are gone; we won't buy your goods. The elected officials that have become bad administrators of our country we want you out. We are going to start looking into every penny you take from anyone. Elected officials and greedy corporations give us back what our fathers and we built.

We owe nothing to China or any other country we have handed our manufacturing and office jobs to. We now recognize our grave mistake and today we will start correcting that mistake. Americans must once again be put in first place. We have let a hand full of people steal the inheritance of our children and give that inheritance to the people in those countries for their children.

Right now we may be still getting by but if we don't change something in 5 years we won't be getting by. China will be getting by splendidly thanks to the U.S. Their children will have a future, but will ours?

Chapter 22

Treaties, What Can We Do?

In the last 15 years, treaties have been signed with countries that allow the trade doors to open wide. When the treaties were signed it appears our leaders may have been acting illegally by accepting money from foreign leaders and foreign companies. Do we still have to honor those agreements?

America is one of the world's biggest consumer customers so dealing with us should be on our terms. We don't have to give away anything to have other countries want to deal with us. We buy their goods and we give them our money, pretty simple. There may be some small segment of the economy that would have benefited from some of these agreements but most of them simply put America in a very bad situation. There was zero benefit to the American economy to allow China and others in the Pacific Rim to take our manufacturing. Giving them our manufacturing and then buying back goods (even if they were cheaper, which they're not) was not a wise economic move.

Right now the biggest war America is fighting is regarding our own economy. The treaties we signed are bleeding America dry. While government economists say it is a good thing to help the world our own citizens are going broke. Our tax rolls are getting depleted at a rate that will hinder even our ability to provide for our armies.

We are in a national emergency that will end up being the

most devastating event in US history. It is way past the time to be polite while our country is heading for bankruptcy. Our worst enemy couldn't have come up with a better plan to weaken America and put our economy in turmoil. We have destroyed ourselves with the treaties that gave away the manufacturing we used to do ourselves.

The idea of a strong economy is to make your own goods and trade to countries that have goods we can't make. The idea of letting other countries take over most of our country's manufacturing is absurd. Now that we have done just exactly that we have to correct this situation. Those countries that now threaten to boycott the USA if we try to put sanctions on imports such as the steel tariffs, so be it. Our concern isn't those countries. Our first concern has to be our own citizens. It is upsetting to think we elected our top officials that didn't understand where their actions were going to lead us. We didn't barter all our manufacturing away; we gave it away.

Cutting back on our treaties isn't going to make us look any worse to the rest of the world than we already do. America seems to have erred in every action we have taken outside the US for the last 40 years. Is it better to sit here and see our country go into severe depression and bankruptcy or to correct the situation? It is way past time for America to save face around the world.

Most countries would respect our decision to start looking out for ourselves, after all that is what all other developed countries do. The rest of the world recognizes we are financially in over our head, which is why the dollar is starting to decline in value overseas. It will decline until we straighten out our act and change what is so obviously wrong. No country can survive if they give away all their jobs.

The treaties we are honoring were ill advised and maybe even illegal. No matter the reason we got into them, we now recognize they will be the death of America. It has to change. Sorry China, you may not get rich on the American dollar after all. If we just let it all slide we will face much bigger problems in the next few years when China becomes the richest most powerful country in the world thanks to US manufacturing. Chinese leaders must be amazed at our stupidity. The global warming that China is causing by making goods for America shows our lack of judgement and it is now effecting the entire world.

Chapter 23

President Bush

When I wrote this book Bush's second term was 2 years away but now that this book is finally getting published Bush has been reelected and we are 2 years into his second term.

During election time what people dislike the most is the pointing of fingers by the candidates of what the other candidate did wrong. Nobody likes people picking on our leaders, and it is with reluctance that I filled this book by pointing the finger at Clinton/Gore and I will now do the same for Bush. I really don't see any way around it, I am trying to tell the reader what we are doing wrong in picking our elected officials and how they get into office and pursue their own agenda rather then the agenda that is best for America.

President Bush is going to be remembered as the president that was in office when our economy went down the tubes. As we now see, the actions of President Clinton would make it hard for any president that followed him. Clinton put in order the course of events that gave away our jobs and he left office before any one noticed the destruction he orchestrated.

I don't know if President Bush is even aware today of the economic events described in this book. I think his advisors are still pointing the finger elsewhere for the economic problems and some of his advisors actually believe we don't have a problem. When Bush declared a tax cut that was a real indication that he didn't have a clue what was causing the economic downturn. It never dawned on him the reason for the poor economy was our jobs were being sucked out of the country at a self-destructive rate. Those refunds he gave of $300 or more per family went right down to Wal-Mart and bought foreign goods. Then that sudden surge of spending made him and his economic advisors think the economy came back.

When Bush was talking about attacking Iraq the polls showed that most of America favored the attack. I don't know whom the pollsters were interviewing, neither myself nor any of my acquaintances felt that way. Our attitude was "we can't do that, America has never attacked any other country unless they were first attacking someone else". Half of America had the opinion like the United Nations, "lets wait and see if we can't solve this thing peaceably". Bush had tunnel vision in his quest for attacking Iraq; he was going to do it no matter what. Some say he wanted to correct what his father Bush Sr. failed to do during the first Iraq war, eliminate Saddam. Now we see why Bush Sr. was a wiser man by not attacking Iraq.

Once Bush pulled the trigger we had no choice but to support him. In any case we must always support our troops. To disagree with Bush does not mean we won't support our troops. What I wonder about is who were Bush's advisors that told him it was necessary to invade Iraq on a rumor that they had weapons of mass destruction? Again it appeared we had a president taking direction from those around him who lacked any wisdom what so ever.

When you are dealing with economics, a knowledgeable man will look at all the cause and effects that may arise before he takes any action. That same thought process is necessary in any of our decisions, small decisions can result in large consequences. Going to war over suspicions, doesn't that sound like a decision made by a 3rd world country in medieval times?

Did his advisors understand that there was no hard evidence there were weapons? Did they understand that they would be the invader and what consequences that would bring? Did they understand they were going into an area with religious beliefs and customs that were thousands of years old? Did they have any idea that much of the world dislikes America? Did they understand that our tax base is being sucked dry by the giving away our jobs and that we couldn't afford a war? Did they look at what the aftermath of the war would be?

Even though Bush and his advisors did not look into any of these questions, half of America had all those questions before a warplane ever entered Iraq airspace. Half of America had all these questions, as did most of the United Nations. Did Bush have a clue about any of the problems he was creating?

It appears our elected leaders think that the American military and America dollars will sway the feelings of the world. Not so. Many countries and most people of the world have a strong dislike for Americans. This dislike of America picked up steam with our involvement in Vietnam. Prior to 1960 America was a country that looked out first for its own people. By leaving other countries alone we became strong and respected around the world. I am not talking about isolationism but just a respect for other countries and their beliefs and have the US come in when we are needed, when we are asked.

Americans have always stood against countries that invade other countries so why did we do it? The world's view of America will be worsened again for a generation or two because we attacked Iraq rather then showing patience and letting the United Nations continue its investigation.

America has preached one thing and done another. We said we hated terrorists and yet now much of the world views us as an invading terrorist nation. We fell into the hands of the terrorists of 9-11 and we stooped to their level. Remember there is no proof that anyone from Iraq was involved in the 9-11 attacks.

By the time this war is over it will cost thousands of Americans their lives and it will cost the American taxpayer 100 billion dollars. This bill comes in at a time America is going broke. Did we learn anything? The American people have never asked our elected officials, to spend wisely. If we have asked them they haven't noticed. They continue to spend like drunks. They are drunk with their own power and feeling of self-importance and consumed with the idea they can change the world into the image of America.

President Bush was no sooner in office when he began going around the country to fundraisers for his own reelection. Why do we allow that? Tell me again how that helps America? Those organizations and companies that contribute are trying to buy influence, why do we allow that? In America each voter has a vote and no one is supposed to be allowed to buy a vote but our current system allows it.

President Bush changed the agenda on the Iraq war into the cause of "allowing Iraq to become a democracy". Only time will tell how that excuse will fly. A democracy is not something you force on a country. Foreigners don't get to invade a country and tell them how to conduct their affairs.

I think Bush Sr. understood why you couldn't dispose of Iraq leadership. It wasn't that he was afraid of Saddam it was because he understood the ramifications of such an action. The religious beliefs of the area alone would have made a wise man uneasy about attacking Iraq. It appears that Bush Jr., like Clinton has trouble acting with wisdom.

UPDATE 2007

The War in Iraq has gone completely haywire. Over 3,000 Americans have died and 500 billion dollars have been spent. The cost of this war is now greater than what we spent on the Korean War and what we spent in Vietnam during that 12 year war. We have been in Iraq longer than we were involved in

World War II. As a result of America overthrowing the leadership of Iraq it is estimated that between 100,000 and 300,000 people in Iraq have died. (With Saddam gone there is no one to stop the religious war erupting between the religions in the area). Hundreds of thousands of people are fleeing Iraq and it is now being suggested that those refugees from Iraq should be allowed to come to America.

One of the oldest countries of the world is being laid to ruble and no one has an answer, but we still have the questions. Bush has been declared the architect of our involvement so we know who got us there and we know almost all elected officials voted to go along with that decision. This entire book talks about the cause and effect of our decisions. We declared war on another country, we deserve what we get, history tells us that. We are now mad at Iran and it is suggested that we attack them because they may be supplying weapons to the insurgents in Iraq. Attacking Iran would be an action that would dig us deeper into the hole we have dug for ourselves. In wars people take sides, we are in their part of the world. If someone attacked Canada or Mexico we would take their side too no matter whom was right or wrong. The chapter on the Monroe Doctrine is coming up and that I think is the best answer we have.

Bush has shown us the power he put into his advisors and none of them were elected, America didn't have a choice. For a long time he was asked to fire some of those advisors and he refused. Should our elected officials have taken action? Those advisors were not held accountable, but then it appears that neither were our elected officials.

I believe Bush had a delusion that he could bring peace and democracy to the Middle East and stop terrorism by attacking Iraq. He implied he prayed before he made his decision. My thought is "What God did you pray to?" Was that the same God the pilots prayed to as they attacked on 9-11? When I pray to the God I believe in my answers are always about kindness, forgiveness, peace and patience. We attacked one of the oldest nations in the world, a nation that is talked about throughout the Old Testament. Bush's decision to attack Iraq may end up killing a million people but he and his small group of followers still believe they did what was best for America and Iraq.

Chapter 24

Rules, What Rules?

When Americans elect officials to fill positions of trust we assume the elected officials will follow basic rules of trust and integrity. The first rule they should live by is to look out for the interest of Americans above all others. The deeds of the last two presidents certainly remind us that our elected officials do not play by the rules we thought they did.

The entire system is being run in Washington under Washington rules. The Democrats and Republicans each seem to have their own agenda, but when it comes down to finances they both seem to share one common goal. The common goal is to stay in office no matter what. They conduct themselves like independent contractors and every decision they make seems to go to the highest bidder. When big business backs an elected official they expect something in return. That "something in return" can be like opening the doors of China to our manufacturing.

There was a time, if someone accepted money it was called a bribe. In my mind it is still a bribe when an elected official takes anything from anybody. In my 27 years as a federal agent we were told to not accept anything bigger then a lunch from anyone. Toward the end of my career they discouraged us from even letting someone buy our coffee. How did we get to the point that our rules on accepting gratuities applied to everyone but our elected officials? We got to that point because those elected officials started making up their own rules. They consider themselves above being an employee, above the law.

By making up their own rules we have a system that allows special interests to control our President and all our elected officials. In the next election for president, Howard Dean has refused public election funds and he will get his campaign financing from anyone he wants. Former VP Al Gore is going to help Dean raise money and of course we know from Gores history that he was an expert in raising funds from foreign companies and foreign countries.

As we saw with the Clinton/Gore team their decisions had nothing to do with what is best for America. Big business and foreign companies and foreign countries took priority over the good of America. We have lost millions of jobs, billions of dollars, and are rapidly depleting our tax base because we have leaders of this caliber. I don't think Americans can survive another leader that sells their decisions to the highest bidder.

We have allowed our leaders free rein, thinking we could trust them. We now see we were wrong. Elected officials with good intentions seem to change when they hit Washington. A few years ago a study was done on about a dozen newly elected officials who stated they would never take money from special interest groups. When they were interviewed 2 years later they had all accepted money from special interest groups.

All our representatives are feeding out of the same trough of "soft money," so how can we get them to change? Maybe if we elected a president that says "enough is enough" and uses his position to put pressure on everyone to change this bribery system we now have.

This ugly situation of letting our officials be bribed can't go on. Howard Dean has made his call that he will be scouring the country looking for contributions so he has made his decision to really suck up the 'soft money' with the help of Al gore who is an expert in the area. I hope you remember that on Election Day. (2007 update Dean didn't win the election, Bush got reelected)

We want rules. We want rules that any employer would expect from his employee. Honesty, integrity and loyalty. The people of America have to stand up and demand this type of integrity.

Even as I am writing this book I see where the party system, the Democratic and Republicans are stating most of the bribery will now go directly to their national kitties. By doing this there will be no limits. A special interest can donate directly to the parties as much as they want with no limits.

This latest tactic reminds us again that you can't close enough loopholes to slow our elected officials down. They consider their agenda much more important than the agenda of looking out for America.

Chapter 25

Walk Down Our Street

I remember seeing an old picture of Eleanor Roosevelt riding down into a coal mine in an ore car. She wanted to get a first hand look at what the coal miners were experiencing in their daily job. Just a few years ago that was the mission of our leaders, to look after the citizens of America. Her husband, President Franklin D. Roosevelt created some great programs to help Americans who were out of work. The TVA, CCC's, and WPA all had lasting affects on workers. Leaders of old seemed to always be concerned about what was best for the average America.

It is hard to say at what point our elected officials decided to look after their own interest first and the American people second. A lot of people think politicians have always been dishonest but it certainly wasn't at the level it is today.

The average American doesn't have any money to give the president or the other elected politicians other than the paycheck the elected official is already receiving. In the past, that is the only wage the politicians asked for. Once the elected officials reach Washington, they have come to expect more than the wages America gives them. We have all been so naïve back home that we thought our officials were working for us, not realizing the impact on our lives the soft money 'bribes' were going to have.

I can't think of a worse betrayal of public trust than what is happening today with the money from special interests influencing our lives, in some cases destroying our lives. Worst of all is when we find out those foreign countries and foreign businesses have bought our elected officials loyalty. Our elected officials have put foreign interests ahead of the American people. To me that is treason.

Our officials run around the world looking for things to mend but they don't have to go that far. Come to America, see the homeless children, see the families that were put out of jobs, see the Americans that don't have health care, and see the tax base changing rapidly so that even the local governments are having trouble surviving.

President Bush, come walk down our streets. Take your eyes for a minute off the rest of the world and off your reelection campaign funds, if you don't you may not get a second term anyway. About one half of America already knows how bad the economy is and what is going to happen if the US doesn't change directions on the exporting of our jobs. To me the biggest issue on your reelection isn't going to be about Iraq, it is going to be what happened to the economy while you were sleeping. (2007 update Bush got reelected for the 2nd term but by a very small margin and he still thinks he was right attacking Iraq).

Chapter 26

China

In the mid 90's the American leaders decided to go full bore into letting China do our manufacturing, lets see what that got the USA 12 years later.

Just about every thing you pick up at Wal-Mart is made in China. The manufacturers have sent millions of jobs to China, which means millions of Americans are out of work. The President of the AFL-CIO Union (Sweeney) stated that the loss of jobs in America is so grave that we can't wait for the government to take action, Americans must start doing something for themselves.

The Bush administration is just starting to suggest to China that America is becoming concerned about the trade deficit between the countries. They are buying a little from us and we are buying tens of billions of dollars excess from them. China's leaders were in the US this week discussing the situation and the Chinese Premier had the following observation on American's concern. He spoke these comments through a CNN news interpreter.

"The U.S. should not be only concerned that the deficit is costing Americans but they should also appreciate the fact it is being very helpful to China and other countries. Not only is the deficit effecting the USA but also other countries. China will try and find more items that our people can buy to bring that imbalance down. We can reach a meeting that will help us all. It will also help if the US will share more of its technology industries."

There was certainly no indication of an apology from China taking all the US manufacturing jobs. After all the USA is the one that came up with the idea. What would China's response have been had Bush been honest and said "The US leaders made a grave mistake and gave China the very heart of the US economy, our manufacturing, and now we struggle in every phase of our economy. China please let us have our manufacturing back." I am sure that response would have met with the same response shown above. China is now in the driver's seat in manufacturing around the world. There is no way they will let that slip away.

The Clinton administration went out into the real world of international economics without a clue that they were playing with the big boys. China is rapidly becoming the country that has all the marbles. The history books will show that the fault didn't lie with China, it was all in the hands of the American government and businesses.

China's suggestion that the USA make more items their citizens can buy is a joke. We can't make any product that they can't make cheaper, but the big difference is their average citizen lives very meagerly and can't afford a higher standard of living. China might come to the US for some big ticket items at first like airplanes, but even big ticket items will soon be copied so that is a short lived thing.

China's manufacturing ability is now so massive their goods are spreading around the world and upsetting economies everywhere. They have the largest and newest factories in the world and they have the USA to thank for getting them so well started.

Can the golden goose we gave China ever be ours again? China will not tolerate the US government imposing tariffs or trade sanctions. Unless we get a president in office that is willing to change things nothing will be done.

China has beliefs that are far different from America. They are taught from childhood to set aside their individual needs in favor of national interest. They are taught extreme work ethics and devotion to their country. Six hundred years ago China was a world leader but then seemed to fade from international significance. They have become a case study of a nation with an extreme population but very little economic development; they are, of course, communistic. Over one fifth of the world population are Chinese. By America giving them our manufacturing we have given them economic relief they could only have dreamed of. By their shear numbers they always knew they should be the most powerful country in the world, now we have made that possible.

While the USA spent the last 200 years developing the infrastructure to bring about the manufacturing and marketing of our commercial and consumer goods China was just surviving. We woke the sleeping dragon. Last year China experienced 25% of the world's entire economic growth and of course we know their growth meant other countries loss, mainly Americas.

The Chinese are now upsetting the manufacturing in most countries of the world. The decision by America to give them our manufacturing suddenly takes on dynamics that effected the world.

The environmentalists were some of the first Americans to try to close down our manufacturing in the name of improving our environment. We sent our manufacturing to a country with no environmental laws. We know where that will lead us. It is just a matter of time before the pollution being created in China will spread around the world. (Update 2007 it is happening as you read this).

As a result of some poorly thought out trade agreements, the US is now sending well over 100 billion dollars a year into

China. What China will do with this newfound wealth will be known in the very near future. It is surmised that much of the government's wealth will be channeled into the military of China. Some people have voiced the view that some of our money will be sent into North Korea to help their military. As time goes on much of the materials they are buying around the world will be used by their own people as they become more developed. When that happens will it leave the rest of the world short of those supplies. (Cause and effect never goes away.)

The U.S. invaded Iraq and tried to set up the same structure that the U.S. believes in, that of a democracy. What can the US do when China invades another country to set up a government system they believe in, Communism?

The US will not be able to do anything militarily if China attacks another country like Taiwan. Our only retaliation will be trade sanctions, that is the only option we will have, we certainly can't go against China with the military, I suspect they may already be stronger than us. If there were a conflict with China where would America get its consumer goods?

Right now America should be reopening all our natural resources and rebuilding new state of the arts environmentally friendly factories. We have to do this now because China has way too much control of our future. We have to take our own future back.

All I keep thinking is, "What were we thinking?" Clinton, Bush and Tomas Friedman may have thought China was no longer a communist nation but anyone that grew up in the 1940's and 1950's never lost sight of that fact. After all those years of fighting communism we simply gave them everything we had. We can't even put into words how dumb it was to give China our manufacturing and to think our elected officials not only allowed that to happen, but they were some of the architects that set it up.

The fact that China is now the biggest manufacturing country in the world would make one believe they are no longer a communist country. They may have changed their strips enough that in the purest since they have strayed from the concept of communism where all property is publicly owned, but I am not sure. Are those manufacturing companies owned by individual businesses or is the ownership just a front for what is really owned by the government? One thing we know for sure is the Chinese government is getting its share of money from those businesses, by either owning them or getting a large amount of taxes from them. In either case the manufacturing of our goods in China is feeding their government, not ours.

We know that the government in China does not respect individual rights and they demand strict obedience to the national authority. If they cannot now be called communist then they will fit into the authoritarian category. The dictionary defines an authoritarian as "dictatorial and tyrannical" so no matter what title you give China they still have the potential to be a government that we shouldn't be giving our America's wealth to.

China no doubt saw what happened to Russia. Russia imploded when they ran out of money because they didn't want to take on a capitalist economy and trade with the rest of the world. China isn't going to make that same mistake; the new China is flexible and will do whatever it takes to survive.

China built the Great Wall to keep people out, but we jumped over the wall to hand them our manufacturing. Only time will tell what effect this will have on the future of the world.

Cuba is a communist country that we are not even allowed to buy cigars from. What a contrast, giving Communist China all our manufacturing and no one says a word. One thing for sure about China is that no one in the US knows what its government is up to and if they are up to no good we won't know about it until it is to late. No matter what they do Americans can't complain because we are the ones that handed them all of our money.

I have just one final question about China. Do you think China wanted to take over our manufacturing and our money to help their citizens, or was it to increase the power of their government? I believe we know China good enough to know the answer to that question.

Chapter 27

Immigration

Immigration is a very pressing issue. Statistics show that hundreds of thousands of illegal aliens are coming into the US every year. In a time of national security concerns this becomes a very big issue. How many of those illegal aliens are coming in with the intent of doing harm to America? We may not know until it is to late.

With all the money being spent on federal employees one would think that an agency that provides such an important task, keeping out illegal aliens, would be appropriately funded. Apparently that is not the case.

We have immigration laws because Americans know how many new immigrants we can assimilate into our country and we want to control the quality of those people coming in. We don't want terrorists and criminals coming in to cause our citizens problems. So why is our government doing so little to correct the situation?

Migrant workers certainly have a place in our country. Our best example is the Mexican laborers that work in our fields. Those workers send home billions of dollars to Mexico each year. They are very efficient workers and for the most part are doing jobs Americans don't seem to want. We want their workers but we want them to come to America legally.

In a time of economic turmoil a bigger question might be "how many more people can America handle when the current citizens can't find jobs?" As the job situation gets worse people will be asking our government to curtail immigration which will certainly require a lot more INS employees to keep our borders under control.

As we all know everyone but the Native American Indian can trace their roots back to another country. Every ethnic group that came to this country added their flavor to our society.

In years past new immigrants to this country prided themselves in trying to quickly become a part of this country. They would learn the language, respect the laws and they went on to become some of our hardest workers. In the early 1900's those immigrants tried to blend into our system and hanging onto their heritage was not a priority. They adopted US customs even to the point they often did not teach their children their native language.

America truly became a melting pot of ideas and cultures but America itself kept its identity with the English language and the over all strong belief in God. In the last couple of decades the trend is going back to people wanting to retain their native countries heritage and customs. While this is very honorable in private or within their portion of the community, it starts to affect others when they force their beliefs onto our society in general.

Until recently, individual immigrants were so thankful to become Americans; they did everything they could to fit in. There was never a question about whether or not they should follow the laws of the United States. We have a very big problem developing in California with illegal aliens that is going to have a dramatic effect on immigration in general. Some leaders in the Mexican communities believe that the illegal aliens should be given the same rights as other American citizens and they are ready to call for a strike for all Mexican heritage people to bring this about.

What those people are forgetting are the laws of our country. No one has a right to come into our land and refuse to honor our laws. The fact that 45% of the California workforce is made up of Mexicans (legal and illegal) does not change the fact that being an illegal alien is against the law.

We can not have any group of US citizens deciding that they are above the law. Come to America legally and my thoughts are "Welcome to America". To come to America illegally and start threatening lawsuits and work strikes does not set well with any American.

People coming to America from other countries with other religions are starting to impact our American way of life. Today I saw a story about the ACLU trying to stop, Christmas Carols being sung in our schools and also questioning whether or not schools can have a Santa Claus. The argument is that not all the children of the schools believe in Christ or Christmas or Santa Claus, so those themes should be banned from school activities.

We all know about Jesus and what Christians believe he did for them but what about Santa Claus? Look in the dictionary and you will see the basis for Santa Claus was Saint Nicholas and he was alive in 300 AD and was a storied gift giver. In the 1700's Santa Claus took on the look of what we see today. For thousands of years young and old have enjoyed Christmas as being a celebration of the birth of Jesus.

Most Christian nations consider Christmas a holiday whether or not every one in that nation believes in Jesus. This joyous time of year goes back two thousand years so why should the greatest Christian nation in the world let a few minorities bring this all to a stop? When I go to a Christmas school play I expect to hear my grandkids sing Christmas songs. The idea that someone might be present that doesn't believe in Christ or Christmas puts them in the minority and they should respect the rights of the majority. If they don't believe in Christmas why are they there?

America is a gracious host to all people and sometimes it doesn't ask for much in return. Some people think that they can live here and have more rights then everyone else, I don't agree with that. To try to take away my heritage of basic things like Christmas Carols and Santa Claus is harassment. I respect those who don't believe in Jesus but I don't go into their lives and try to stop their beliefs or customs.

(The amount of money the illegal aliens are sending back to Mexico each year is peanuts compared to how much we are sending China each year but is still part of the draining of the American economy.).

UPDATE March 27, 2007

I just read today about something that is being proposed by the administration. Have you heard of the North American Union? This involves building a super freeway from South to North across Mexico, through the US and across Canada. This would open up the borders and appears to be almost an annexation of Mexico and Canada for most purposes. We would have one coin called an "Amero" similar to Europe's Euro.

What I read doesn't say anything about how it will effect the immigration of people but an action like this will certainly open up more doors for coming into our country. From what you hear about Mexico, with all its corruption, drugs and crime I don't know if America can afford this whole scenario. If the Mexican borders are opened up how many millions of Mexican people will flood into America?

My question is how do American citizens gain by this project? It sounds like we may not even be able to vote on it, how does that sound? It certainly sounds great for Mexico.

Canada and Mexico aren't strong military allies but there will come a time when we may have to protect our North American Continent so we might as well get used to it. When China has the military might to control the world it may be in our best interest to retreat to our area of the world and leave the rest of the world alone. I hope the new superpower doesn't come in an attack the US because they don't like our president.

Chapter 28

Homeland Security

America is worried about homeland Security. But most Americans are not yet aware of the potential danger of giving away our jobs and the devastating destruction that our spiraling economy can bring to our national security. If a terrorist can't blow up our buildings the next best thing is to destroy our economy and weaken our entire system. Giving away our jobs seems to be doing just that, destroying the financial base of our country.

The reason we are so strong militarily is because we have had the finances to pay for this great arsenal we have. The war in Iraq will cost us well over 500 billion dollars and we have military forces spread all over the world. This all comes at a cost, a cost that a declining economy may not be able to afford.

Shutting down our of natural resources, closing our factories and sending our money overseas to buy back our consumer goods can have some terrible consequences. These actions have greatly cut into our tax base and have reduced our money available to spend on the military. I know Washington thinks we can just print more money and borrow on our future to pay for their spending today, but that is a very unsound principal to operate on.

Aside from not being able to pay for our military as our economy goes overseas, there are a lot of other side effects. All the US manufacturing plants are either closing to go overseas or are getting rundown and aged. We are no longer self-sufficient, that makes us vulnerable.

We worry about terrorist weapons being brought in from other countries but we are letting thousands of ship containers come into our country every day. Go to any port, especially on the West Coast and watch foreign containers being unloaded onto our shores. The checking of those containers are minimal compared to the volume of goods coming ashore from all over the world. Most of those goods should be made in the USA and not brought into this country. (That alone would help eliminate the possibilities of terrorist items being brought into the US.)

Contrary to our leaders thinking, there is an end that will be reached. The government attitude of "spend and damn the cost" is something we can no longer tolerate. They are putting our country in grave danger by allowing these events to continue. Bankrupting our nation is by far the most real and dangerous threat to our homeland Security.

We have to get our elected official's attention and convince them that their loyalty isn't to their contributors but to the 290 million Americans that elected them. How can we, as Americans get their attention? Patriotism doesn't seem to work because if they were patriotic they would not have sold out to outside interests to begin with.

One of the things that comes to mind, for the public interest is to file a lawsuit showing that the exporting of our jobs is putting our homeland security in danger. That would be easy to prove since we are sending hundreds of billions of dollars overseas each year. Someone with no education and only knows how to keep his own household budget can understand the math in this situation.

What about the rest of the world, how will they feel? Leaders in other countries, who put their own citizens first, certainly understand. As we see the value of the dollar going down overseas we know part of that reason is because those foreign investors know that the US is bankrupting itself by exporting our jobs and having a military that we can no longer afford.

To protect America, we are going to upset the countries and companies our elected officials sold out to. We can live with that to keep America strong. But the hard chore is going to be with our elected officials. We are treading on their playground, on their status, on their commitments to special interests, on their ability to stockpile money for their reelection.

Homeland Security must start at home. Our leaders must take measures to keep our economy strong and that is their number one mission at this time. But we all know they will not change their ways so it may come down to America taking action without them.

I understand about half of the money the US has borrowed came from overseas interests including China. Does that sound like a good policy? Americans themselves can't raise enough money to support our government. Does that tell us something? How does that fit into our national security?

When President Roosevelt said to "walk softly and carry a big stick" we should have listened. Our inept foreign dealings have gotten the US in over our head.

How the rest of the world views American leader's attitude toward other countries plays a very big part in our national security. Many people around the world hate Bush and it is only a matter of time before some of them come into our country to due harm to our leaders because they have a fear that we might attack their country next. By attacking Iraq every country now views America as a "Lose Cannon" that has the potential of doing damage anywhere in the world. I just hope no other country attacks us using the American attack plan of "Let's attack them before they attack us".

Americans have a tendency to not understand other people of the world. We seem to have "educated arrogance"; both Clinton and Bush fit this stereotype to a T. Since WW11 we have viewed ourselves superior to all other countries. For a lot of years we had all the trappings of the best country in the world. We think we have become the world's leader, but no other country in the world has the same opinion of America that we do we do of ourselves. The guns and money we spread around the world did not buy anyone's loyalty or respect.

The average American may not understand how much the rest of the world dislikes Americans. I encourage each reader to go to any country in the world and see how the people there respond to you as an American. I have seen pictures of handouts in Ireland showing Bush as a war criminal, so be prepared to face reality. Americans aggressions around the world are starting to catch up with us. It appears the attacking of Iraq was the final straw to everyone watching the ease that America goes off to war.

In 1968 Sirhan Sirhan, a Jordanian-born Arab, assassinated Robert Kennedy. (I remember that well because that was the week I graduated from college.) In an article I read about Sirhan he stated that he was afraid that if Kennedy got elected as president America we would attack his country. The probability of scenarios like that occurring again are going to be more likely as the US becomes more hated and feared around the world. We can blame our elected leaders for this course of events, but remember we elected them and keep them in office no matter how badly they go astray.

Muslims are doing most of the terrorism that is occurring around the world. Their dislike for America intensified when we attacked Iraq. The religious war that is erupting in Iraq would not be happening if the US had not destroyed their entire government. Our officials are now trying to blame Iran for the continued violence but we can only blame ourselves. As usual the American officials that declared this war take none of the blame.

Chapter 29

Let Things Stay as They Are

When we look at the problems we have and how much effort it will take to correct our situation a person just feels like saying, forget it we will let things go on as they are. Nobody likes to whine about his or her situation and we really don't like people talking about our elected officials. I know that feeling. That is what I thought when I kept putting off writing this book. I don't like hostility.

When we get weak-kneed, let's just remember what our elected officials did to us. They took away our future. They have not been good employees. Many of them need to be fired. The entire system they created for themselves has to be reviewed. That entire system will get nothing but worse and someone has to step up and say, "we've had enough".

The first week I went to work for the IRS a speaker came in with the following comments. "If you find a violation of the laws you are upholding and you decide to walk away from that violation without taking any action, then get back in your car, drive back to the office and turn in your credentials because you are worthless to the organization." Those words stayed in my mind for the 15 years I spent as an IRS Agent. I was tempted a few times to walk away from my audit findings, but I never did. What is right is right. Will we walk away from this impending catastrophe or take some action?

We have a system in Washington that allows people to buy the ear and votes of our elected officials. To me that is a crime. If we don't stop it there will be no end to it. With the system that is in place, it is getting harder and harder to get those in office out.

The bottom line is, they gave away our economy, or should I say sold our economic system for their own personal gains. Our sons, daughters and grandchildren depend on this generation to safeguard their heritage. If we ignore these happenings, we are saying their future means nothing. If we do walk away without attempting to right the wrongs, we should be ashamed of ourselves.

No one wants to dig up the Clinton/Gore days. By the time they got out of office we were sick of hearing about them. Those two had no memory of wrong doing even when they were still in office so by now they won't remember getting a single penny from anyone.

Why can't we let the whole thing go? Because Clinton and Gore are still out there and still involved in various phases of our election. Gore raised money for Dean in the last election. Clinton has a wife that is running for president. These people are not going to go away, but at least we can try to keep them at a distance. There is no doubt that there are other elected officials that have the potential of becoming what Clinton and Gore were so we have to let all elected officials know we will no longer tolerate that type of activity. We also have an opportunity to tell our corporations that if you don't like Americans enough to make American goods then we won't buy your product.

What can we do? We can make a stand against letting things go as they are.

Chapter 30

Globalization

I have talked about globalization throughout this book because it is going to affect each person in America for the rest of our lives. It sounded so good in theory because most people thought that it would involve encouraging each country to increase it's own manufacturing and provide the consumer needs for their own people. The computer age would also allow them to get their goods on the world market. We would now be one big happy world where everybody gets ahead.

The reality of globalization didn't work anything like the average American anticipated because of one very important issue. Those countries weren't expected to create anything for themselves, they were told they could just take America's manufacturing and then America would buy back the consumer goods we used to make for ourselves. Those 3rd world countries would simply attach themselves to the American economy. American factories would close down and new factories would be built in China. Workers in India could take jobs that American's used to have using the telephone or computers and all they had to do was learn to speak better English.

I mentioned that Thomas Friedman's books THE WORLD IS FLAT and LEXIS AND THE OLIVE TREE are great reading about how great globalization was going to be. He went to many countries talking to their leaders and found that everyone was so excited to become part of the worlds trading field. He wrote that the days of war and threats of war are over because we are now one world due to the computers and cell phones. (He wrote the books before the US attacked Iraq).

His story is great, his research was exceptional, except for one thing, he forgot to walk down main street America and see what the economic effect would be on American workers, especially blue-collar workers. He failed to consider the economic impact on any country that stops developing their own natural resources and manufacturing and sends all those jobs to the underdeveloped countries. He states that anyone who does not buy into this program will become "turtles" and "road kill".

Mr. Friedman doesn't have an economic background so it is understandable that he didn't differentiate between the types of jobs being sent around the world. It is one thing to export jobs that can be done on computers and telephones, but it is quite another to export the jobs that relate to a country providing its own consumer goods. It is the dream of every country to be able to provide their own goods and become self-sufficient. For the most part America has been manufacturing it's own consumer goods for two hundred years. Now, in 15 years we have given almost all of it away. The multiplying effect of jobs and their importance to an economy providing its own consumer goods were never discussed in his books. I believe he simply did not know enough about economics to understand what effect his books would have on America.

I didn't talk to dignitaries around the world like Mr. Friedman did, but my work experience allowed me to talk to the people that mean the most to America; the blue-collar and white-collar American workers. Apparently the thought process of Friedman and Clinton were the same, they both bought into this great "One World Globalization" theory. I understand Friedman is now rewriting THE WORLD IS FLAT and I hope he puts in a few pages about the destruction globalization has done to America and he should also mention that communism didn't go away after all.

When history looks back at America, I believe the most important single thing that changed America is Globalization. We know that the Clinton/Gore era ushered in this entire concept and brought it to a level that resulted in the destruction of much of the American workforce and our manufacturing system. The Clinton/Gore team was very aggressive in getting contributions for their reelection campaign but the exact details are still murky. We know some foreign businessmen and possibly foreign governments contributed a lot of money to the reelection of the Clinton/Gore team and others of our elected officials. The parties involved will not have any memory of doing this nor will they have any recollection of even knowing what was happening.

Clinton gave speeches indicating that he thought American was going to become an exporter of technology and become a service country. He was not aware that the American economy still needed manufacturing and blue-collar jobs. He thought those menial jobs were better suited for developing countries.

The concept of allowing our manufacturing to be done by other countries needing work sounds honorable, but only for a second. A person with any knowledge of what makes an economy work would have vetoed the idea as soon as it was presented. We are now witnessing what is happening in China as a result of America giving them our manufacturing. They are putting rockets into space. They now have US money rolling into their country by the billions and they are just starting. China is now a manufacturing giant, building new factories everyday, but in America our plants are closing down. Who has the brighter future? Prior to the Clinton/Gore connection China could have only dreamed of such riches.

The second party to this globalization scam is American businesses, they knew by opening up places like China they would have access to the cheap labor and cheap materials to produce goods for America. I don't think they could have expected to sell US type goods to the general Chinese population since their standard of living is so different from ours. What the manufacturers got out of the deal is that it allowed them to abandon their US manufacturing plants with all the labor problems, production costs and environmental issues. It also allowed them to bring in consumer goods at a fraction of the cost and still sell their goods at US made prices resulting in unheard of profits to the company.

America may want to have the rest of the world look and think like us but it is not going to happen. The religions, traditions, diseases, warring factions, poverty and lack of basic human necessities all come into play and rich America isn't able to bring them all up to our standards with this globalization concept.

When we complain to companies about sending US jobs overseas the response is "We have to so we can be competitive" and "we are doing our part to become part of the global economy". Once you see the overall picture and see what damage the idea of globalization is doing to America those excuses no longer hold any value. It was a scam generated by foreign countries, American businesses and American elected officials and nothing more. But there is always an exception to the rule so they can point to a few segments of the economy that have been benefited. But we must go back to rule #1 we must do what is best for the majority of America.

It would be interesting to know who the first person was to coin the word globalization and in what context he thought of the word. It may have been a humanitarian viewing the riches in some countries and the poverty in others. He may have been thinking about how each person and each country could do more to improve the lot of the poor and sick no matter what country or what race or religion a person was. I bet the person coining the "globalization" phrase never meant it to be an excuse to export many working class jobs out of America and give them to a communist country.

Poorer countries have always thought rich countries like the USA should do better at sharing their wealth. Globalization is like a worldwide socialist concept, spread the wealth around the world. The problem is that the ones paying the bill are those working class American people that lost their jobs. The US Government is also paying dearly by its decline in all phases of the tax structure.

When you hear of what former President Jimmy Carter is doing, the word "globalization" takes on a different meaning. He is going around the world as a peace diplomat; he is personally participating in helping the sick and the poor in many countries. He is giving the best of himself to help the needy. If we all had his attitude we could each be giving a little to stop the problems around the world. I don't think giving away American jobs to communist countries, or any other country is the way to accomplish this goal.

Contrary to what Americans think of themselves, a lot of the world views us as greedy, self righteous and spoiled. Some even think of America as Satan. Those people who so dislike us must now be looking at our situation in amazement. The most intelligent of terrorists could not have created a plan so delightful to them as the one the Clinton/Gore team put in effect and is now being continued by Bush. By giving away our jobs and stopping most of our natural resource development the tax base will be so deteriorated that before long America won't be able to pay for our great armies. By sending our money overseas to buy our basic consumer goods we have turned America from a self-sufficient country to a country dependent on the rest of the world for our goods. By China producing a lot of our goods it puts this communist country in a position of power over the US. They have our jobs, our money, and yet they didn't have to give us a thing in return, apparently just pay our elected officials some "soft money" for their reelection campaign.

For Americas sake I would hope everyone would veto the globalization idea by simply putting back on the shelf anything not made in America. Let us get our jobs and our wealth back and then start helping the needy around the world. Let us elect leaders that understand what it means to look out first for America.

Globalization worked great, just as they planned, for businesses, foreign countries and our elected officials. I believe we can agree it is also working out great for Communism. It does not appear that a single one of those people involved in this idea understood a thing about economics, they certainly didn't understand enough to know what effect this would have on America.

I am setting here looking at my round globe of the world and as I turn it I can see the countries of the world in just a few minutes. The map of Africa has so many countries and as I read the names of each country I get visions of what I have seen about each one of them on TV, countries like Zaire, Zambia, Kenya, Nigeria, Ghana, Ethiopia, Sudan and Zimbabwe. They all sound like exotic far away places, but as the TV always shows there are some terrible things happening in those countries. Death, starvation, aids, drought, tribal wars, disease, genocide, orphaned children and the list goes on of what daily life is for those people. Zimbabwe seems to be a typical example of what is taking place in Africa. Twenty years ago they had one of the strongest economies in Africa, but today that country is in shambles and turned into a police state by the black leader of the country.

The people we see in those documentaries about Africa have one thing in common; they are all black. Is that why the rest of the people of the world seems to ignore trying to help those people, because they are black? They wanted to rule themselves rather than have white involvement and it does not seem to be working. China is now going into those countries with US dollars and I so wish them well, those people need help so badly.

Just a slight turn of the globe and you are looking down at Iraq, a small little country a half a world away from America. In this 21st century America, the most advanced country in the world, is there involved in possible the most insane war in modern history. The destruction we are causing in Iraq of both lives and property lets us know that this grand theory of a one world, cell phones and the Internet doesn't bring peace after all. The cost to America so far is 500 billion dollars but that is nothing compared to what the poor people in Iraq are suffering with the daily terrorism by both the American military and the insurgents. To a family losing its loved ones it makes no difference who did the killing, it is terrorism. When someone terrifies you by destroying your life all you want to happen is for it to stop. But who is going to stop this war? Americans still think we have the right to be there. Most of that area of the world is Muslim, which as a group do not seem to think much of America, and when we invaded their part of the globe the hatred for us intensified.

Just another twist of the globe and you can look down into Vietnam. We don't have to say much about that war, but we should take a minute to remember 58,000 Americans who died there fighting Communism. America walked away from that war in 1975 leaving all of Vietnam to the communists.

Spin the globe just a little further and you can find India, China, and Thailand, an area that is now producing a lot of goods for the US. The American dollar is needed there so much because of their poverty which looks as bad as the poverty in the African nations. This is where most of the US dollars are going since they are now manufacturing all the US consumer goods.

As we keep turning the globe we see the countries of the Americas. South America has its areas of poverty and unrest and some of the countries like Venezuela are even starting to dislike the US.

And then of course you have our little country of America, a place that historically has devoured more than our share of the world's goods. America is a consumer country and in the past we got away with our excesses. Today our buying habits take on a different meaning for a very important reason; we no longer manufacture our own consumer goods since most of our goods are manufactured in other countries.

I wish America had done more in the past to help the poor of our own country and the poor around the world. I wish we hadn't spent so much on war. I hate poverty and I hate war.

The jobs we gave away are helping other peoples in other lands. It is helping Communism; it is helping make some people rich in other countries. It is helping some workers in those underdeveloped countries but the average citizen in places like China and India will never see a penny of our money. I understand one of the richest men in the world now is a man in India who is involved in bringing jobs to India from America.

In the world there is about 6 billion people. A large percentage of those people around the world are living in poverty and the US giving away our jobs and shutting down our natural resources will not change that. I wish it would.

Around the world there are many countries that are controlled by tyrants that are far worse then Sadam. I hope we now understand that going into those countries and starting a war is not in the best interest of anyone.

I sincerely hope that if unrest comes to America or if another country doesn't like our president that they do not attack America like we have other countries.

No matter what we do we are not one world. We do not have the same agenda. When you look at how Africa has imploded since black leaders have replaced the white rulers you can see that many good ideas just never result in doing what is best for the people. I was so hoping that it would work for Africa, in the entire world they need the most help. When you watch what is going on there it seems the entire continent is going to implode.

The point I am trying to make by looking at the entire world is that the giving away of American jobs will not help the world become one big happy place. The weakening of America by this action will only put one more place on the map that will start deteriorating. To be a caregiver for the rest of the world we must remain strong and that requires getting our jobs back. China is about to surpass America in wealth, power and world control and we don't think they will be a reliable caregiver, but it was our decision to make it happen.

Cell phones and computers have made it so we can all connect with each other and has allowed us to share each others technology, but those items appear to have nothing to do with world peace. America has shown the world that even if every person has a cell phone and computer their leaders will still take them to war. Until computers can tap into the mind of each countries leaders no one really knows the terror that leader is plotting. What are the leaders of China planning right now with all of the American dollars they have received? We don't know, we can't even guess. What country is Bush now thinking about attacking? We know Bush would love to attack Iran and if he does will the American people remain quiet like we did with Iraq?

A few people in America decided to stop our natural resources development and send our manufacturing to countries with no pollution control. That decision is now polluting the world.

Shouldn't we apologize to the rest of the world for that action? Shouldn't there come a day we should apologize to Iraq and the rest of the world for attacking Iraq? Shouldn't we apologize to the rest of the world for the squandering our wealth while much of the world is starving to death?

Shouldn't our leaders approach every conflict with dialogue and diplomacy rather than with guns? America it is time to take the blame for our actions. That is how you bring about world peace. If America is supposed to be a world leader it is time we started acting like one.

Chapter 31

Signs of an Imploding Economy

Have you ever heard the phrase "Trade deficit?" That means that we are purchasing more goods from overseas then they are buying from us. The end result is that billions of US dollars each year are leaving our country and not coming back. Earlier I mentioned that America is imploding, this is one of the reasons that is happening. We are going broke because we are exporting just our money and importing of our consumer goods. America as a country probably has the biggest trade deficit in the world. It appears that in spite of this trade deficit the government and our economist still feel our economy is strong.

Economists point to the stock market to show how strong our economy is. Every time a company states that it is transferring it's manufacturing overseas the price of that stock goes up because everyone knows the profits of that company will now skyrocket. When and if they bring their manufacturing back to the USA their stock price will go down because their profits will fall. They will have to spend money retooling and building new factories in America.

Housing costs have gone up at a tremendous rate the last 15 years. Much of that increase is due to the increased costs of building materials. China has become the manufacturing giant of the world so they are now buying up the worlds supplies of gas, steel and all goods needed to supply their factories. The war in Iraq increased the demand for building materials as we try to rebuild what we have destroyed.

The number of houses being repossessed in 2007 has increased dramatically. Some economists suggest it was because the interest rates were to low, in the last few years it had dropped down to the 5% level. Many of those loans were at a variable rate so as the prime interest increased those loans went up and so did the payments. As a result of this many people have to turn back their houses.

Here is another thought about why this happened. The price those people had to pay for their houses were double what they should have been had the cost of housing materials not gone up so much. I see the connection, not only in interest rates, but also another side effect of what China has done to the price of materials.

Another overall problem is many blue and white-collar workers losing their jobs around America. The jobs they lost paid a lot more than the jobs they are now able to find. They are unemployed or underemployed. They have to relocate to find jobs; their living standards have fallen as a result of their declining incomes. Sometimes they had to just "walk away" from their new house. All these events will have an effect on America's economy. Bringing back our factories and reopening our natural resource development will help us rebound but things will keep getting tighter until we do.

The value of the US dollar is going to continue to go down around the world. The rest of the world knows all about the grave mistakes we continue to make, giving away our manufacturing, the growing trade deficit, and the money we are spending going off to war. They view us as a rich nation that is out of control and we have elected officials that show no sign of changing our course.

Chapter 32

India

When you mention "outsourcing", India comes to mind. They have many employees that are well educated and speak very good English ready to do Americas computer and telephone work. They are gaining momentum every day and there are already a half million American jobs that have been lost to them in this outsourcing project.

It is hard to say where to start when we discuss India. It is one of the world's poorest countries so it seems greedy to say we don't want them to have our jobs when they are so poor. John Lennon used to take trips to India to be reminded of how lucky he was to have his wealth. When we think of India we think of poor children scavenging through the dumps, stinking smoldering dumps, to get enough to eat. We can only hope that giving away of Americans jobs can alleviate this situation.

India is the second most populated country in the world, behind only China. Trying to raise their standard of living, is very honorable in theory, but is giving them our jobs going to help the hundreds of millions of poverty stricken people of India? When you read about India there are usually comments about the rich natural resources they have, but they are not developing them. You read about the farming potential they have, but they are not using modern tools to maximums their output.

India is a country that needs help. There is no doubt of that. Why aren't we trying to help them develop what they have themselves, rather than just giving them our jobs? The average American knows what that answer is, give us our jobs back and when we have extra we will help. Unfortunately, that is not what is going to happen under our current course of events. We hope our elected officials understand the situation of Americans needing those jobs as bad as the people of India do. As we already know our elected officials spend a lot of time with these countries deciding Americas fate so we wonder whose side they are on.

Once the US started dealing with countries like China and India and sending them our jobs, those countries started to become more outspoken about this process. They want to keep those jobs and fear the US will rise up and stop this outsourcing. Here is what India is doing about it. Let me quote a story in the paper on 1-18-04 put out by S. Srinivasan of the Associated Press. It comes under the headlines "Officials say outsourcing won't hurt U.S."

"Indian politicians and business leaders now fear those gains could be in jeopardy. They've taken alarmed notice of a brewing grassroots backlash in the United States where companies are replacing software developers with Indians who earn roughly one-sixth of what the U.S. workers command."

Continuing "And so Indian leaders have moved beyond marketing their country as a global technology hub. They are now promoting the economic benefits of transferring technology jobs to low-wage workers in the developing world. N. Chandrababu Naidu, chief minister of India's southern Andhra Pradest state, a top outsourcing designation for US corporations, recently met a group of visiting US congressmen in Hyderabad and urged them to defeat anti-out-outsourcing regulations."

"Outsourcing cannot be stopped," Naidu said "we know it and they know it."

"Some economists say Indian officials should not worry so much that their lucrative outsourcing revenue stream will dry up. They're convinced that cost savings will trump any fledging backlash in the West."

Do those statements make your jaw get a little tight? India officials urging our US elected Congressmen to defeat anti-outsourcing regulations. Ah—excuse me sir, our elected officials are put into office to look out first for America, not India. In days not long past, our elected officials would have come out of meetings like that with large contributions in their reelection kitties, I hope that didn't happen here or we are in real trouble.

Just as troubling as India's attitude that outsourcing can not be stopped, is the insight provided by one of our top economists, a Noble Prize Winning College Professor. He thinks 50 million more jobs will be created in the US. Pie in the sky economists like that are who our administration must be listening to. Where are these new jobs? Any new jobs would also be subject to outsourcing. It all appears to be a one-way street, to other countries and out of America.

The backlash of speaking out against outsourcing hasn't built up steam yet, but it will as soon as US citizens understand how it is destroying their country. We want to help other countries but we want to help other countries on our terms, not on theirs. To India and any other country that wants American jobs we say, "go develop your own jobs." Americans have worked too hard for the last two hundred years to develop our economy and our businesses to just send our jobs out without a fight.

We know the businesses that are outsourcing have no conscience about this. It saves them a lot of money. The companies that are doing this are noted in this book and that list changes daily. I would hope each reader would look down that list and stop doing business with them. They are turning their back on the American people.

For India officials to tell us the outsourcing can't be stopped, makes me want to organize America to make it stop. For the American companies that are doing this, I am ashamed of you all. I have dealt with many of the companies on the list and I have yet to see their fees decrease to reflect the savings they are getting by selling out American jobs.

To understand India, take some time and research this great, vast country; it's religions, customs and it's government. It is the only democracy in Asia. What is written about the country makes it clear that a lot of their problems go back to the very things that make it so unique, it's religions and customs. It was mentioned earlier about how Christian nations seem to develop into stronger countries because of people being able to work well even though they may have religious differences. That appears to be one of the many problems India faces. I understand the Caste system is outlawed but still exists.

Researching back on India it appears that the US has been giving them a great amount of financial aid. Going as far back as the early 1970's the US was paying the bill for about half of the cost of their government, even then America was sending them a 500 million dollars a year. What I could find mentions our help to pay for their government but it doesn't mention a lot about the US trying to help them to develop their agriculture and natural resources. Like the old saying goes, "Help a man plant a seed and he will feed himself, feed him and he becomes your dependent."

We know India has a lot of problems that they themselves have difficulty fixing. Religion and customs stops some of their development so the easier solution to them was to simply take American jobs. Most Americans don't think that is the answer, let them develop their own economy.

China has a billion people, India has a billion people, America 290 million people and yet we are giving them our jobs. Can't we see that we are fighting an impossible situation? We can not bring them up to our level; they have to bring themselves up without taking our jobs.

We shouldn't blame India we must blame the Americans that set up this globalization concept.

Tell the half million people who have already lost their jobs to India that it was a good deed.

Chapter 33

Accountability

In the real world if an employee makes a grave mistake he is fired. Why doesn't that same principle apply to government employees, including the elected officials? Each year employees of the government make grave mistakes and yet not one single person loses their job. Why is that?

No matter what position a person holds they have to be held accountable. By accountable, I don't mean just saying "I accept responsibility" and then keep their job. Janet Reno accepted responsibility for the Waco mishap that caused so many women and children to die. Did she resign? No, nor did a single person lose their job. If you accept responsibility and your action caused extreme damage to others then you should resign.

Before the 9-11 attacks, Federal Investigators and private flight instructors were trying to warn their agencies that Middle Eastern students were acting suspicious by wanting to learn to fly planes but weren't interested in learning to land them. The agencies notified failed to take action but no one received a reprimand let alone actually having a person relieved from his or her position. Clinton had taken action so that the FBI and CIA could not share information, but since that time Bush has changed that law.

Each scenario gets more serious. We are involved in a war that most Americans didn't want, nor did the world community want and yet President Bush went ahead with his plans. Now that no weapons of mass destruction were found Bush agrees an investigation should be made to see what went wrong with our intelligence. It is time to stop this insanity of not taking responsibility. President Bush that was your call. You called yourself "the decider" and it is you that must be held accountable. Don't now start looking for who else to blame, it happened on your watch. Hundreds of thousands of people dead, 500 billion dollars spent and no end in sight and still not one politician resigned or even suggested it was their fault.

Americans are tired of our officials passing the buck. Everyone knows who made the decision to go to war and that person should step aside. Bush has a lot of good traits and was the man to fill that position when 9-11 occurred, but he let his decisions get side tracked to a personal vendetta. He wanted to get Saddam.

Bush has a chance to bring a lot of respect to being an elected official. He can resign and accept responsibility for the killing of so many people and at a tremendous cost. Nixon resigned and what he did was nothing compared to Bush. Let other elected leaders get the point that if you screw up the American people want you to leave and make room for a more competent leader.

In the military service when you are on guard duty you are responsible for things that happen "On your Watch" You take very seriously every thing that happens when you are in charge. That sense of being responsible is totally lacking in our government leaders, it is time to make people accountable for things on their watch. This book spelled out the events that went haywire on Clinton and Bush's watch but neither will admit to anything.

My fear with Bush is that he will take us into another war before he gets out of office.

Chapter 34

World Trade / Free Trade

Since the beginning of time, people and countries have traded with each other. That is certainly a time-honored tradition that began when countries found their way to other's shores.

People have always wanted to trade for those things we can't make for ourselves.

Americans have been intelligent enough to have worked hard to develop our manufacturing process. The lives, money and time that went into developing our manufacturing abilities can not even be measured. Manufacturing was Americas golden goose providing us with one of the best standards of living in the world.

In days past no one in their right mind would have suggested that America close it's factories and send the production of our basic consumer goods to another country. I hate to keep repeating this but I am in shock that we let this happen. To let all the jobs and money go to China, a communist country, goes beyond anything this world has seen in the 3,500 years China has existed. This decision will forever effect the rest of the world.

I think the key is to let goods come into America but not those that cost Americans their jobs. No more importing "American brands" that used to be made in America. Maybe even stop all our imports until this national disgrace is corrected.

Trading goods is one thing, closing our factories and taking the entire factory to another country and buying back those products is a different story.

I am happy for the rest of the world that they have come into the age of computers and now have the ability to go online to reach every country in the world. The problem I have is they have side stepped creating their own economy and simply attached themselves to America's economy. They have learned English, learned to use the computer and built factories to reproduce American goods, all at the expense of the American worker. I don't feel like they are doing their share by simply taking American jobs. What have they done to earn our jobs? Why must American blue and white-collar workers pay the bill?

I doubt if there is another country in the world that would close their own manufacturing plants and give up their self-sufficiency to hand it over to another country. Their leaders are smarter than that.

Chapter 35

Social Security

Every day the news has stories about concerns of depleted funds in social security. There has not been a single mention about the fact the jobs going overseas are creating much of the problem.

Having spent 15 years as an Internal Revenue Service Agent I am very familiar with all phases of taxes. Every thing I say about taxes applies to taxes of all kinds, Social Security taxes and income taxes, all taxes that derive their source from products and labor.

As hundreds of thousands of jobs (maybe now even millions of jobs) are sent overseas it represents money not going into social security. Politicians may think that doesn't affect anything because people losing their jobs just go out and get another job. That is not so.

As we should all know by now, the jobs lost are quite often high paying jobs. A displaced person may end up working for half the wage just to find work. All unemployed and underemployed people have a direct, immediate effect on social security. You can apply the same rule to people paying their income taxes.

When the US brings all the jobs back from other countries many of the social security problems will be solved.

Social Security was originally described as "any system by which a group provides for those of its members who may be in need:" specifically, in the United States...old age. When social security is put in jeopardy the ones hurt the worst are the elderly, the very ones that helped create this great nation that this younger generation has given away. The tone certainly is about helping the needy. To millions of Americans Social Security is the only retirement they have and it is being drastically damaged by our current actions.

Remember the "work-chain" we looked at earlier where one job creates many jobs? The consequences of eliminating the work-chain that runs from raw material to the retail store is severely felt in the coffers of all phases of the government due to reduced payments into the tax system including social security.

The social security taxes are sent into bank accounts at least each quarter. The decline of those taxes coming in show up very quickly. I can't imagine the impact to the social security bank accounts from the loss of hundreds of thousands of jobs.

Our spending polices are going to bankrupt this great country. The spending habits of our country have to be brought back under control so it matches the income it receives in taxes. For every 100 private sector jobs sent overseas a government job should be eliminated.

Our tax system has to be changed both on income taxes and social security, but most of all what needs to be changed is the governments spending habits. The government is staying in place while the benefits given back to the people are being cut back.

Chapter 36

Companies Outsourcing Us Jobs

The worst enemies we have are the ones here in our own country that sell out the American worker and take our jobs overseas. When we buy a product it is easy to read the label and see that it was made elsewhere and we can put it back on the shelf. But what about those companies that are now sending our office jobs overseas? They are harder to identify. Following is a list of those companies we know are outsourcing office jobs to overseas, mainly India. CNN.com compiled by Lou Dobbs provided this list on the Internet. Remember this list changes daily.

3M
Accenture
ACS Affiliated Computer Services
Adaptec
Adobe Systems
AMD
Aetna
Agere Systems
Agilint Tech
AIG American International Group
Akin, Gump, Strauss Hauer and Feld

Alamo Rent A Car
Albertsons
Alliance Semiconductor
Allstate
Alpha Thought Global
American Express
American Standard
Amphenol Corporation
AOL America On Line
Applied Materials
AT&T
A.T. Kearney
Avery Dennison
Bank of America
Bank One
Bechtel
Best Buy
Black & Decker
BMC Software
Boeing
BP
Burlington Northern Santa Fe Railway
Capital One
Cendent companies as follows:
Amenhost Inn
Avis
Budget
Century 21
Cheap Tickets
Coldwell Banker
Days Inn
ERA
Fairfield
Galileo

Travel Port
Howard Johnson
Jackson Hewitt
Knights Inn
Lodging.Com
Ramada
RCI
Shepard Business Intelligence
Super 8
Travel Lodge
Wingate Inn
Cerner Corporation
Charles Schwab
Chase Morgan
Chevron Texaco
Ciena
Circuit City
Cisco Systems
Coca-Cola
Comcast Holdings
Computer Associates
CSC Computer Sciences Corporation
Continental Airlines
Convergys
Cooper Tire & Rubber
Cooper Tools
COVAD Communications Group
CSX
Cummings
Daimler Chrysler
Dell Computer
Delta Airlines
The Democratic National Committee
Direct TV

Discover
Dow Chemical
DuPont
Earthink
Eastman Kodak
Eaton Corporation
EDS Electronic Data System Corporation
Electroglas
Eli Lilly
EMC
Emerson Electric
Ernest & Young
Expedia
Exult Inc.
Exxon Mobel
Fedders Corp
Fidelity Investments
First American Title
First Data
Fluor
Ford Motor Company
Franklin Mint
Gateway
General Electric
Hewlett-Packard
IBM
International Paper
Intel
JP Morgan Chase
Microsoft
Oracle
PeopleSoft
Prudential
The Republican National Committee

Siebel Systems
TPI
TRW Automotive
UTC United Technologies Corportion
Wipro Technologies

Chapter 37

The Iraq War

When I started on this book in 2003, the Iraq War had not yet begun. I didn't think it would happen because it was so contrary to everything America stood for. Never in U.S. history had we invaded another country because we suspected they had weapons of mass destruction. I was confident that our leaders were smarter than that.

Our leaders apparently felt threatened by Iraq and felt we should invade them before they invaded us. I am not sure where that paranoia came from, we knew we had the military might to wipe that country off the map if we so desired. Most confusing was why we felt so threatened by Saddam. A lot of people thought it was more a matter of what President Bush wanted to do, and that was to go in and finish the job his Dad had not done.

We had already shown Iraq our power in Desert Storm. We had Saddam contained and isolated. We were so much more powerful then Iraq, so why invade that country? The first President Bush felt that leaving Saddam in power would be better than the alternative of extreme unrest that might occur if he were eliminated.

Americans still wanted to fight back at someone because of 9-11-01. We picked Iraq in spite of the fact there was not one single hijacker from Iraq. Any connection, at best, between Iraq and 9-11 was circumstantial. Hidden weapons were only a suspicion.

Anyone who has spent any time over seas or has had any dealings with a Middle East country know their entire thought process and religious beliefs are far different from the American way of thinking. We surely wouldn't invade a country without fully understanding the ramifications of our actions. Would that country's population really want U.S. involvement? Would other Muslim nations accept anything we set up?

Should any country under any circumstance attack another country based on suspicions? The U.S. has not liked to see any country invade another because we know history does not look kindly on acts of war. The invader always comes up short.

My only thoughts prior to our invasion of Iraq were "please America, don't do that". We already knew what the outcome will be, another Vietnam with a twist of religion. Aggression is an ugly thing no matter who does it.

Half the U.S. population still seems to support President Bush. We have forgotten the weapons of mass destruction and we have developed an attitude of "Oh well we still wanted to get Saddam" and we got him. We did find some mass graves of a few thousand people. I am reminded of how Saddam got into power in the first place; didn't the US put him into power?

We have now moved our thoughts away from weapons of mass destruction to the fact that we were able to get voting done and Iraq is now a democracy. Let me see, who was it that gave us the authority to invade other countries and set up our way of thinking? Don't we get upset when other countries try to do the same thing? When Hitler wanted to take over other countries he invaded them. When Russia wanted to expand their ideals an invasion was always in order.

A democracy is a thousand times more than just the ability to vote. To most of those people a democracy actually goes against their religious beliefs. Women don't seem to have any rights under their religious law and it doesn't appear that a democracy will change that. Most of the people they showed on the news in the lines to vote were woman. Sure we would like to see woman around the world have rights but who are we to mandate that?

The democracy we have in the US has a basic principle that may never be able to occur in Iraq, the separation of church and state. It does not appear that can happen in any nation of Islam because Islam is above all other things. If your religious beliefs dictate that women have no rights but in a democracy women have equal rights you can't have it both ways. The US has no right to ask a people in any country to walk away from their religious beliefs.

The insurgents that are coming in from other countries to blow themselves up in Iraq don't like America or what we stand for. Could it be that the reason they hate democracy is because a democracy goes against their basic religious beliefs?

When we look at how countries have a way of correcting themselves there is no better example than the Berlin Wall. Who would have guessed that the wall would come down, not by warfare, from outside invaders, but by the will of the people within their own country? History has shown that in the long run that is pretty well how it works.

It appears half the people of Iraq liked Saddam and the other half welcomed the change. But those who wanted change, did they know we would destroy so many of their people and their country to bring about this change?

Our actions reinforced most of the world's view of America. They view us as an aggressive arrogant country, some even view Bush as Satan himself.

Couldn't we have better shown the benefits of a free society and a democracy by trying to spread help and aid around the world? As former President Jimmy Carter stated. 'The world had so much compassion for the U.S. because of 9-11 and the world was ready to stand behind us to fight terrorism, but our invasion of Iraq has voided all that good feeling and support'. Well said President Carter.

Before a country invades another country it must always weigh the good being done with the cost. The decision by Bush to invade Iraq was poorly thought out. No thought was given to the fact we had no right to invade another country. No thought was given to the actual war and the aftermath. No respect was given to the people of the area, as to their wants and beliefs. No thought was given in regards to the lives that would be lost both American and Iraqi. No thought was given to the financial cost, billions of dollars. Billions of dollars that America doesn't have. No thought was given to Americans own homeless and poor with medical needs.

Do I support the troops in Iraq, you bet. They went there under the order of the Commander in Chief. Young military people are giving their lives; we owe them a lot. But we don't owe respect to our leaders for taking America into a war that wasn't necessary and wasn't our right to instigate.

We started off saying that we were scared about the weapons we thought they had. When that didn't pan out, it was about turning Iraq into a democracy. Both of those reasons related to US agenda, not an Iraq agenda. We are blowing up a country, killing their people, turning the entire region into turmoil because of US agenda. The US does not have the right to make it our agenda to turn a country into a democracy, period. We didn't have a right to kill their leaders and destroy their cities. The events of 9-11 didn't give us that right.

UPDATE *July 2005*

The war in Iraq goes on, and on. The US press calls the people going into Iraq blowing themselves up, civilian insurgents, Bush calls them thugs. But in the minds of the people blowing themselves up it is their religious beliefs that drive them to such sacrifice. Fortunately, most people believing in Islam consider those suicide bombers radical because they are not following the Koran.

When President Bush was considering going to War it was implied that he went to church and prayed a lot before making his decisions. I believe Bush considers himself a Christian. To me any leader that implies he is praying to God to decide to attack another country, and then attacks it, is mentally incompetent whether he calls himself a Muslim or a Christian. Any time an individual or a leader believes that his God wants him to react to a situation violently I certainly wonder about whom his God is. I consider myself a Christian and the God I follow would never have made me feel in my heart that it is appropriate to attack anyone for any reason. Some Christian churches still follow the old testament of an eye for an eye but to be a Christian and follow Jesus most people feel you must follow the teachings of Jesus and never return violence with violence. When someone wants to do his own will just say so, don't suggest that your God told you to do it.

UPDATE December 2006

I am still trying to get this book published. The war is still going on only now the real statistics are coming out. We have now been in Iraq longer than we fought WW11. The estimates of how many Iraqi civilians have been killed or injured in Iraq range from 300,000 to 700,000 people. The US causalities are about 3,000 with about 30,000 seriously injured and that figure is growing daily. Iraq now appears to be in a civil war with religious factions fighting each other. The US government is starting to have hearings trying to decide what went wrong. They have to look no further than the day they decided to invade that country. People that study the Middle East know that area is one of the oldest in the civilized world. President Bush thought he could go in and change that area by wiping out their leadership and setting up a democracy. What is shown on TV is a country that is being destroyed by America.

President Bush still will not concede that he may have made a mistake. I am reminded of a statement one of the newsmen made right after America attacked Iraq, "I hope President Bush is right because if he fails all Americans fail". At this point the war has cost over 500 billion dollars that the Americans have had to borrow. We failed Iraq, we failed the world and we have failed ourselves.

When the war first started I was talking to an old WW11 veteran that had never before mentioned that he had been in some major battles during WW11. Fighting back tears he said, "if President Bush had ever seen war he never would have sent our solders to war". Americans just have to watch it on TV, those people in Iraq, the children, woman, young and old have to live in terror, terror caused by us, the Americans. Young American men, some only boys, continue to die daily and only Americans have the power to stop this insanity.

There are now protests in America both for and against the war. It is Vietnam all over again. I remember in about 1965 we had already lost about 3,000 soldiers when people started wanting us to get out of Vietnam. Part of America wanted us to stay so those 3,000 didn't die in vain; we stayed until 58,000 had died in vain. We are proud of each one of those that gave their lives but we are ashamed of our leaders who put them in that position.

Some people may argue that we had to go into Iraq because there were some terrorists hiding in that country. There are terrorists around the world in many countries like England, France, Canada and even in the US. That is what terrorists do, they go into the civilian population and blend in until the time comes for them to commit some terrorist act. We can't blow up the world trying to get to those groups or individuals.

My views now appear to be "second guessing" the war but my views were expressed before we invaded Iraq but I couldn't get anyone interested in my book. The effect of the war on the US is extremely small compared to the effect on the US of giving away most of its manufacturing to China and other countries. The next chapter explains why I was against the war before it started.

In my opinion there is nothing in this world more insane than war, period. If the leaders of one country want to fight another country take them into the desert and let them kill each other.

But that isn't how war works they want to go into each others country and kill woman and children and destroy all the buildings in sight. They want to use up all the resources they have to destroy another part of the world. Every country has limited resources so war takes away from feeding the poor, healing the sick, educating the next generation and making the world a better place to live. Leaders that take their country into war are idiots and should be replaced as soon as they suggest war. Leaders of old understood diplomacy and dialogue, two things American leaders seem to not understand.

Chapter 38

Founding Fathers Monroe Doctrine

On December 2, 1823 the Monroe Doctrine was implemented. That document spelled out a policy that remained a guideline for the US until this generation. It told the rest of the world that the American continent was no longer to be viewed as a location that other countries might lay claim to.

That document further states that the US would not intervene in other country's parts of the world unless the United States is threatened. "It is only when our rights are invaded or seriously menaced that we resent injuries or make preparation for our defense...

"The political system of the allied powers is essentially different in this respect from that of America. This difference proceeds from that which exists in their respective Governments: and to the defense of our own, which has been achieved by the loss of so much blood and treasure, and matured by the wisdom of their most enlightened citizens, and under which we have enjoyed unexampled felicity, this whole nation is devoted. We owe it, therefore, to candor and to the amicable relations existing between the United States and those powers to declare that we should consider any attempt on their part to extend their system to any portion of this hemisphere as dangerous to our peace and safety. With the existing colonies or dependencies of any European power we have not interfered and shall not interfere. But with the Governments who have declared their independence and maintain it, and whose independence we have, on great consideration and on just principles, acknowledged, we could not view any interposition for the purpose of oppressing them, or controlling in any other manner their destiny...Our policy in regard to Europe, which was adopted at an early stage of the wars which have so long agitated that quarter of the globe, nevertheless remains the same, which is, not to interfere in the internal concerns of any of its powers:...But in regard to those continents circumstances are eminently and conspicuously different...It is still the true policy of the United States to leave the parties to themselves, in hope that other powers will pursue the same course..."

This document was addressed to the European countries. As stated in the Avalon Project at Yale Law School. "It is still the true policy of the United States to leave the parties to themselves, in hope that other powers will pursue the same course."

The US invaded another contrary to the US principles. Do we think we have a right to invade another country, on another continent while we ourselves would not allow that to happen? What are we going to do if someone invades Mexico under the belief that it is a threat to their country? Then when the threat proves to be wrong try to change their government system to that of the invading country. How would we feel?

Didn't we experience this when Russia tried setting up missiles in Cuba in the 1960's? We didn't tolerate that action. Why do we now believe we have the right to do that in Iraq? We act as if it is the duty of the US to spread democracy though out the Middle East.

A democracy involves so much more than the right to vote. The democratic system in the US worked because of a thousand things including our religious beliefs. The very nature of Christianity requires we work well with our neighbor so those principles alone make a tremendous difference. The fact that we developed a free market system, a tax system, a government structure that has endured for 200 years. All this makes for a democracy and it all happened over a period of time, it wasn't as a result of another country invading us.

To go into a country and force them to be a democracy over night is absurd. When we went in to Iraq and destroyed the ruling section of that country we violated every intent of the Monroe Doctrine.

Our founding fathers had wisdom far beyond what we see in today's leaders. Their ideas were well thought and their ideals have endured for 200 years. Our leaders today appear to lack wisdom and understanding. In the Monroe Doctrine it is mentioned that other countries have their own agenda and their own polices that we will not impose on as long as they leave us alone.

The events of 9-11-01 did not give us the right to attack another country. We knew almost immediately that it was not a specific country committing this crime but it was members of a terrorist group from several countries, none of which was Iraq.

The leaders we now have in the US seem to think we have the right to do whatever we want around the world, to those leaders I say "go back and read the Monroe Doctrine". There was a reason for that wisdom. Those leaders knew right from wrong.

The main obligation we have to the rest of the world is to show them the advantages of our system. By attacking Iraq we showed the rest of the world that is okay to attack another country based on "suspicions" and that once we invade that country we then have the right to destroy their system of government and kill and imprison their leaders. We then have the right to set up a political system that appears to be contrary to the beliefs of the region and contrary to the religious beliefs of the area.

Our leaders are trying to rewrite the rules on how Iraqis should live. But it will turn out to be a very destructive attitude.

We will now witness other countries doing the same thing, invading other countries on suspicions and then trying to impose their will on the dominated country.

The Monroe Doctrine tells us to leave other continents alone. What about the fact that we sent most of US manufacturing to China? I really don't think our founding fathers would have liked that, because they had wisdom. Don't tinker with other countries and they won't tinker with us. Our wise founders understood "cause and effect" before the phrase was coined. If you wonder about the statistics and effects worldwide read the March 2005 copy of the magazine Inc., on the front cover it says "China Shock". We are finally waking up to the danger of the bed we crawled into, both in China and Iraq.

Our elected leaders no longer even discuss the question of whether or not we should have invaded Iraq, mainly because most of our elected officials went along with Bush. Now the only question is how do we get out of this mess and save face. I would like to express some views on getting out.

The first thing to get straight is that there is no saving face for America. We made a grave mistake and the world knows it. As Jimmy Carter says the world felt sorry for us after 9-11 and then hated us when we attacked Iraq.

To come up with an answer to how and when to get out of Iraq I might present a scenario. Let's say in 10 years China is far more powerful than America and they decide to attack our country because they don't like our President, they think he is a threat to them and are afraid that America might attack them so they attack us first.

They come and destroy our capital and either capture or kill all our leaders. The country goes into turmoil as China tries to set us up as a communist country. After a few years they decide it was all a mistake and want to get out of America. They are afraid to leave because they think we will self-destruct without any national leadership. Our citizens have split between Christians and Muslims and we start killing each other.

Now here is the question. Should China just exit the US or should it stay around for a few more years while they try to decide what to do with our country? The fighting is going to go on whether they stay or go.

Is your vote to have China stay in our country, even though both the Christians and the Muslims hate the Chinese occupation?

Or is your vote to have China leave immediately and let Americans recover as best we can, but China must pay for all the damages they caused.

Before you answer remember what happened in Vietnam, one day America just packed up and left. We knew staying would just prolong the bloodshed. We still remember the picture of the last helicopter flight out of Vietnam and those that had been on our side were struggling to get on board. Many of them were killed as soon as we left. It was harsh, but I believe in the long, run lives were saved. We shouldn't have been there to start with and again we find ourselves in exactly the same position, only this time the damage we have done to Iraq appears worse than what we did in Vietnam. In Iraq we wiped out their leadership as well as their country for no justifiable reason. (Do you remember we were in Vietnam fighting Communism?)

What is your vote? Do we stay in a country where our presence is causing hundreds of deaths a week or do we pack up and hope they work it out on their own? Before we go we will tell all the people in Iraq that America will pay to help them recover.

To answer that question let's go back to what we want China to do after they attack us and now want to leave. Do we want them to get out of our country today or do we want them to hang around for a few years in the hopes that things will get better?

My vote to both questions is "JUST GET OUT." Leave Iraq just as I would want any country that attacks America to do, just get out. Americans just don't get the point, that part of the world hates the US and the longer we stay the more the hate festers.

Our president Bush is a hated man around the world, do we want another country to attack America and destroy our country because they hate our leader? That is what we are doing.

The stories coming out of Iraq about the good the US has done there are few. What have we done to help their private economy become part of the world society? Do countries like Iraq even want to be part of the world society? Friedman wrote in his book before the Iraq War started that there has never been a war in a country that has a McDonalds restaurant. He notes that two countries that do not have a McDonalds are Iran and Iraq. He thinks in this new one-world global economy there is no room for war. Little did he know that this great country of America would start the next war.

As we try to get things solved in Iraq some of our leaders say we should send in more troops.

That reminds me of the old "dig us deeper" mentality of Vietnam. What I haven't heard is our leaders talking about diplomacy and dialogue. Bush refuses to talk to anyone in Iraq that might be considered our enemy so any negotiations seem to be out the window. I say get all the power brokers in Iraq together and lets start talking about how to turn this destruction around. I don't care if that person has power because of being a religious leader or a military leader, however he holds influence, bring him to the table. Have Congress elect a spokesman to represent the US. Bush and Rice have always turned down dialog and they don't seem to have an understanding of the situation, so don't send them.

Remember what Kissenger said "never turn down a chance for dialogue with anyone". Eventually America has to get out of Iraq and when we do whoever has power will start running the country, the fact the US doesn't like their future leaders won't change that fact. We got rid of their last leader, what are we going to do if we don't like their next one?

Chapter 39

France

There was certainly uproar by many people in America when France did not want to join Bush in the war on Iraq. I hope some thoughts I have on the subject helps you forgive France.

We all know that France gave us the Statue of Liberty, which is the second most important American symbol we have, behind only the US flag. I can't think of any other country that has given the US anything. To me that is a very big deal. I sailed past the Statue of Liberty on a troop ship on my to Germany during the Berlin Crisis in 1961. I was 18 years old so I know first hand what the feeling is when that lady comes into view. In my case, I didn't see America again until I was 21 years old. I love her and everything she stands for, and forever I will be thankful to France for giving her to America.

During the Revolutionary War, on February 6, 1778, France was the first country to acknowledge America and signed a treaty with us and pledged their military support to fight the British. They sent troops and that may have been what allowed the US to win the war. If it wasn't for them we may have remained under English rule.

I am one of those old fashioned people who believe a friend is forever a friend. If a friend has a different opinion then I, so be it. When France didn't want to join the US in the war on Iraq many

Americans became outraged. There was another time that the USA and France did not agree.

When Johnson inherited the Vietnam War from President Kennedy America was only starting to get involved. There were some casualties but most people in 1963 were not even aware of Vietnam. Those of us in the military at that time considered the US's involvement in Vietnam as a President Kennedy conquest, he was trying to find a place to fight communism. Communist North Vietnam was starting to invade South Vietnam. Remember that was Communist China's neighborhood so they supported North Vietnam.

When Johnson started to escalate the US involvement in Vietnam, there was one country that tried to advise America not to get involved, that country was France. France sent a delegation to the White House to see Johnson to advise him to keep out of Vietnam. Johnson refused to see that delegation and the rest is history. We went on to have 58,000 Americans killed and we can only wonder what the result would have been if we had listened to France. France came to the table with first hand knowledge of Vietnam because they had been fighting there for years (it was a French Colony) and knew the people, the terrain and the quagmire that awaited the US if we kept our involvement there. After taking heavy losses in Vietnam, the French finally moved out and of course the US moved in.

When France didn't want to go to war with Iraq they knew what lay ahead, they didn't want to get involved in another Vietnam. Their refusal was based on what they knew and felt about getting involved in the Middle East. They had the same feelings that a lot of Americans had. It is a no win situation when one country invades another. To me, France was acting as a friend to America just as much, or more so, than England who willingly joined in the fight.

I was in France from 1961 to 1964 while stationed in Germany. That was only 16 years after WWll. One thing that impressed me as I traveled between Germany and France was the fact there were still bombed out buildings, visible in France, but Germany showed no signs of war. Germany was rebuilt and going strong while France still seemed to be struggling to get past the war. Germany was the invader so you would have thought that it would have been the opposite.

I know the US lent France some money after the war, but I really don't believe we did much else to help them. Germany was another story; the US went in and helped them rebuild. We had a very large number of military occupation troops in Germany which itself helped the German economy a lot. We had some troops stationed in France but not many.

Some of the worst battles of both WWI and WWII were fought in France. France was in the wrong place (Between Germany and England) and their country and people suffered immensely for it. One walk through the graveyards in France will tell you how that country suffered as a result of war. The devastation France suffered during those wars was a million times worse than the attacks America suffered on 9-11. They know the results of war better than any other Christian nation. Their homeland was a battlefield with no regard to the fact they didn't want war. When they were invited into the war with Iraq they turned down the request and were thankful they had the option to take it or leave it. How many wars throughout history were fought on French ground? They were sick of war and they didn't want any part of being an invader to start another war. The wise statesmen of Americas past used to hold to those same ideals. Bush unnecessarily panicked and France wanted no part of that.

What most Americans do not know is that in WWII the French gave up to the Germans after just a few weeks of fighting, they simply didn't have the military to fight off the Germans. The Germans then occupied France until the Allied Forces came into France to drive out the Germans. Much of the destruction of France came about when the Allied Forces started bombing the German military throughout France. Even with their country destroyed the French people were elated that the US came to liberate them.

Today France and England both are experiencing terrorist actions in their streets. This shows when it comes to terrorism; there are no rules.

For the most part, I found the people of Europe to be wiser in their decisions than Americans tend to be. Most of them are at a place where most Americans can only dream of being, just left alone. Had America been being attacked by another country there is no doubt that all of Europe would have jumped in to help, including, and maybe especially, France.

I wanted to add this chapter to remind us all that France is still a friend, they have done a lot for the US and we have done a lot for them. They have been both the invaded and the invader in wars. They have came to the conclusion that both these scenarios should be avoided when at all possible. Their vote to us was to wait until war was the only option available. I respect that and only hope that America can someday find that wisdom.

Chapter 40

Islam

The religions of the Middle East are so far different from Christians, or any other religion. The militant members of Islam are setting a standard of terrorism and violence that is shocking the world. What really makes it shocking is that we can watch it live from our living rooms. These people are killing themselves and everyone around them and doing it with the belief that their God is in full approval of their actions. They are protecting their region of the world from America. American boxer Muhammad Ali refused to be drafted during the Vietnam War in the name of Allah, he is Islamic so we know they are not all violent.

Attacking Iraq was so full of errors in the American leaders judgement. Maybe the biggest error was not understanding the people and the religions of the area. We already knew many Muslims believe America is Satan so we should have known that any thing we try to do there was going to face resistance. Our founding fathers may have known that when they told the world "you mind your business and we'll mind ours". They knew it doesn't work to invade other countries and we will go to war only in self-defense of our piece of the world.

We couldn't have picked a country to attack that is any more opposite to America than Iraq. There is one similarity though and that is the belief that God wants war. Our President Bush implied that he prayed before calling for the attack, which means he feels his God, ordered the attack. The early days of Christianity was known for its violence, with an attitude of "if you don't believe as we do we will kill you".

I really don't know much about Islam other than what I see on the news but the more I read about the Shiites and the Sunni's they sound like they have very similar beliefs. I have heard that they are like comparing Baptists and Catholics, very close but different rituals and doctrines The Middle East has been warring for thousands of years and they seem to be full of hate so their future may continue that way.

What do I think about the Muslims? They don't believe as I do on anything but I vote to leave them alone, especially their countries. When they come into our country they have to follow our laws. If they come in individually or as a group into our country and try to do us harm then treat them as terrorist.

What are we doing in their area of the world? It has been said many times, "The only reason we are in Iraq is because of oil". I do believe that. We have killed hundreds of times more Iraqi's than Saddam did so we are their greatest enemy. Americans should get out tomorrow and quit pretending we had the right to attack their country. To stay is just to prolong the turmoil. Open our pocket books and be prepared to reconstruct their country. This will cost Americans all the money we have in our pockets and then some, money that should have gone for Americans health care. Also, finally admit that we were wrong and promise the people that our leaders will again read the Monroe Doctrine and never attack another country again unless we are asked by the United Nations to get involved. Get out of Iraq before we decide to attack Iran as part of the deal.

Chapter 41

To the Victor Goes the Spoils

The more industrialized a country is the more it demands the supplies needed to run its manufacturing plants. In the past America has been the manufacturing giant of the world so we always got first bid on the goods needed to make products like gas, steel and building materials. When we stopped utilizing our natural resources and closed our factories that all changed.

We opted to have China become the manufacturing giant of the world and with that decision comes the consequences. China is now going around the world buying up gas, oil, steel and all the building materials needed to feed its new manufacturing role so now in America we have to pay more for all those goods. This is another basic cause and effect economic rule that our government economists didn't take into account when they were blue printing this globalization concept.

This has to be the first time in world history that a country had the ability to provide for itself and instead opted to turn all that over to other countries and import almost all their durable goods.

The "Spoils" goes to China, what they are now reaping by winning this Economic War is hundreds of billions of US dollars each year to spend on whatever it wants. It can spend the money we give them on their military, to buy up gas and oil reserves and steel around the world. They can go into Africa and help that area develop their natural resources that will go to aid China. They can raise the standard of living for many of their billion plus population. Oh, what a dream came true for the biggest country in the world. They recognize that all the power and money America had will now be theirs. Now that was a reward worth fighting for, but wait, they didn't have to fight for it America just gave it to them.

Communist China watched Russia fail because of lack of funding. China was smarter than that, so they took on the look of a capitalist country. The damage to America by losing this Economic War to Communist China may not show up for a few more years, but it is guaranteed to show up. Another "cause and effect" that Clinton and Friedman never considered.

In 100 years China will dominate the world and America will be just another place on the world map.

In the Iraq War there are no winners, only losers, so there will be no spoils.

Chapter 42

Exit Plan

I view the events described in this book as the most destructive events to ever take place in America history. Our wealth is being given to China. Our national security is greatly at risk because we have closed our manufacturing plants. We can not continue at this pace and expect to have a strong America in 5 years or 10 years. We have given away our future and the future of our children. Our fathers and grandfathers would be ashamed of this generation of Americans.

We could gather together all the environmentalists, politicians, and business people that made this happen and put them in prison, but that would not change a thing. We have to play the hand those people gave us. They represent less than 1% of the population but the other 99% have to find a way out of the mess they created. People like Clinton, Gore and Bush will never admit in their lifetime they made a mistake and all we can do is try harder to never elect people like them again. Let's find leaders with wisdom with an understanding of economics.

When you start any endeavor there has to be an exit plan, a way to survive when plan A doesn't work. Can we agree that shutting down our natural resources and sending our jobs overseas may have been wrong? Is it too late to change things? I don't think so, but if we don't change, those actions could bankrupt America.

To get America back to being self-reliant again requires us to go back to producing our own consumer goods. We must first start again to harvest our own natural resources. Open back up the mines and forests since these provide the natural resources that would let us open our factories. The rules for harvesting our natural resources should be based on the technology available today to avoid as much as possible future pollution problems.

We must insist that our environmentalist cooperate with the program. They must learn to understand the entire harvesting process. They must come to understand that trees are a renewable resource that can and must be harvested. We can not allow a few people to shut down logging when they have no idea about the importance of harvesting. We also seem to have government workers in place that are short on knowledge of what prudent logging should look like.

The mining of our minerals should be done with the utmost care to avoid pollutants and that can be done with our current knowledge. We must acknowledge that mining is a good thing, it provides us metals that are necessary for every day life. It provides us metals for our national defense. American smelters are closed; they are now across the border in Mexico and China.

We must do the mining and logging with the idea that by us producing these goods in the US it not only provides for our financial welfare but it also stops the need to get those goods from countries that will pollute the world.

The Government must set a timeline. After a certain date no more manufactured goods can be brought in from other countries. The only goods that can be brought in will be goods that America can't make for itself.

Set a date two years from now, a drop-dead date of January 1, 2009. After that time all imports will stop. The two-year time frame would allow the US to open up its mining and logging, build new factories and transfer the business operations back from China and other countries. This would have ripple effects in the US; it would give us immediate jobs in rebuilding our manufacturing community. It would give the world notice that the US is finally coming out of a deep sleep and will look out for its own citizens first. Right now, the US dollar on the world market is dropping daily. The rest of the world recognizes the problems we are having. Immediately you will see an increase in the value of the US dollar.

All manufacturers will be on notice that the goods they sell after that date can only be made in the US. This will give them incentive to bring their manufacturing back to the US. The 2-year wait will allow them to use their massive profits to rebuild here.

We don't have to apologize to the world for what we are doing. Most of them were no doubt surprised when we allowed this to happen in the first place. All countries but the US seem to look out for the welfare of their own people first. In America our countries welfare was put last.

America can survive two more years of this insanity of giving away our manufacturing, but we don't want to go beyond that point. It is imperative for our national interest.

To pass a measure like this will require a fight. Remember that most of our elected government officials have already been paid by big businesses and foreign countries to be allowed to take our jobs, so there will be a fight. Everyone will have many reasons why we shouldn't do this but the only reason Americans need to have is that it will save our country.

Plan B and maybe the one I most believe in is for 290 million Americans to write to the Walton family that owns Wal-Mart and ask them to implement the 2 year requirement that all goods sold in their stores must be made in the USA. This scenario is a workable plan. Wealthy people can get things done. The American government can't or won't. I intend to send the Waltons a copy of this book.

Chapter 43

America vs. China as World Leader

In the last 14 years the biggest transfer of wealth and power in the history of the world occurred and not a shot was fired. America got robbed and beaten by the politicians during the Clinton run. We witnessed generations of work destroyed in a very few years.

Bush had his own agenda it seems, right from the start. Bush also sees himself as a world leader, his arrogance and demeanor is the view of America that foreigners have. Full speed ahead and damn the consequences. The Clinton decisions were the most damaging in US history but on a single event in US history nothing will prove to be more damaging to the US than Bush's decision to attack Iraq.

Right now Bush feels like he will change history by spreading democracy. He gave no thought to the destruction that he would put upon Iraq. He gave no thought to the religions in the area and he definitely gave no thought to the fact you don't spread democracy by war.

America continues its war games. We continue spreading weapons around the world to our friends (who sometimes turn out to be our enemy). We continue to hand out money around the world, that money usually goes into the pockets of the countries corrupt leaders. We continue to think the world views

America as the world leader. We are the only country in the world that thinks we are great. Lets accept the fact that in recent years our actions gave credence to what a lot of the rest of the world thinks, "Americans are idiots".

So much for America now lets look at what China has accomplished while America was being lead by Clinton and Bush.

China convinced our leaders and our businessmen that it would be good to let them do the US manufacturing. Hundreds of billions of dollars a year are being pumped into China from the US. This action is sucking America dry and making China rich. My, what a unique concept. What a way to turn the tide of power.

Now lets look at what China did with the money. We know they are building up the military in China and North Korea with some of the funds, what about the rest? An article in the Wall Street Journal on March 29, 2005 spelled out in detail what China did with part of the money.

China went into Africa and started doing things that would appear to be for the people, like building schools, building roads, putting in power lines and helping them develop their natural resources. I bet they never took a single rifle into Africa. What a unique concept, go into a country and do good things.

China didn't try to spread communism right off the bat; they come in knowing that they will be repaid by the spoils of the natural resources they will bring out of Africa. The money China will make from those African natural resources will add fuel to making them the most powerful rich nation in the world.

China had three things going for them as they went into Africa. #1 they weren't American. #2 All the money they made by taking US jobs financed this African project. #3 they didn't go into Africa trying to force anything on them. They didn't try to force their doctrine. They didn't go in with guns blazing.

America we have been out shuffled, out maneuvered, outsmarted and it has cost us dearly. No, the American leaders are not world leaders. Bush and Clinton became pawns for the rest of the world.

Unfortunately the actions of our elected leaders from 1990 to 2007 caused such change around the world and especially in America that it may take several generations to recover. America is solely responsible for turning the sleeping dragon into the most powerful country in the world. Our leaders won't accept that charge but we can see it is true.

Chapter 44

China and Pollution

As noted in the March 2005 copy of the Inc. Magazine the first clouds of toxic waste has hit the California shore. Lou Dobbs did a story in the last week of March 2005 showing the severe pollution in China. This pollution is beyond our worst imagination and it is spreading around the world. There is no question, in the global warming issue; China is one of the major causes.

I have talked to several people that spend time in China and they say they are also polluting the rivers and the ocean. That type of pollution will also spread around the world. We have been warned that the fish in the ocean are starting to have large amounts of mercury in them.

We have to do all we can to encourage China (and the rest of the world) to clean up their act. China especially must be told. They are no doubt smart enough to know how to correct the problem, to them maybe the reason they don't is "the bottom line". It costs money to change things.

China should be approached with information about the health of their people. What they save by not stopping the pollution will be spent in health care. Does China even have health care?

Suggestion: Bill Clinton is a hero in Asia because he gave them the US jobs, make it his project to convince them to clean up their act.

China is in a position to do tremendous good in Africa but they can cancel the good by polluting that great continent.

America tried to do away with its pollution problems by having all their consumer goods made in China, but it backfired on America and the world.

The cause and effect of sending our jobs and manufacturing to China is as follows:

1. American economy is in turmoil
2. World polluted by China
3. America tax base in the red
4. China is becoming the most powerful country on earth
5. China is buying up gas and manufacturing materials so they are skyrocketing in price.
6. Most of our factories have been closed so in the time of national need we can not even make our own goods.
7. This action created the biggest transfer of money and power in the history of the World. Transferring from a democracy (America) to a Communist country (China).

As an American how does this make you feel? Do we want this to continue?

Who are the best world leaders? Based on the above Communist China beat America real bad on just about every count. We don't know about their world leader ability, we won't know that for another couple years when they will have the strongest military in the world.

Chapter 45

What Could Have Been?

Every country has its own people, its own religion, its own standard of living; it's own work ethic and beliefs. America doesn't get to dictate to any other country. Maybe the best we can do is set a good example and if other countries like what they see, follow our example. We can encourage and help them, but historically we have taken what appears to be lot of wrong turns.

I see in 1989 we lent Iraq one billion dollars to buy American goods. What do you suppose happened to that money? Did it go into Sadams palaces, the Iraq military? Saddam was already killing his own people and committing atrocities. Was it smart to send them one billion of the US taxpayers money for any reason?

Our elected officials do things like this consistently. We choose a foreign country, send their leader a lot of cash and it always comes back to bite us. Don't you wish we had taken a different approach years ago?

A lot of countries are still in a 3rd world economy due in part to the way they themselves conduct their business. Many of those countries have leaders like Saddam who hoard any money that comes their way, yet the US keeps sending them our money. We pick sides in areas we know very little about and end up sending them arms to go along with the cash. America has become one of the biggest arms dealers in the world and now as those arms are turned against us we wonder what happened.

Is it too late to do what we should have done at the start, help with each countries basic economy. Help them develop their own natural resources, teach them how to grow better crops and how to manufacture their own goods. If each country were self-sufficient, what a boost that would be to the citizens of those countries. Instead of sending them cash for their leaders to horde send them machinery to farm and manufacturing equipment and send them our experts to show them how to utilize what they already have. Or is it time to just leave every other country alone?

If we had we been helping the countries themselves and truly helping their people the entire world would now be a better place. The people in each of those countries would know how much help the US was and what a kind generous people we are.

For hundreds of years the development in these 3rd world countries were done by companies from countries like America. The real spoils of that development didn't go into the country itself; the real profits were then taken out of that country. Lets stop that by helping each country develop their own natural resources and let them keep their own profits. The days of colonization are over.

What I am talking about in this book isn't isolationism. It is simply being smarter about how we deal with other countries. I think it is time for the US to think about America first. If we have excess we share, but we must share wisely. No more sending our money to corrupt leaders and arms to countries to fight their neighbors when it is not our fight.

We are rapidly finding out in Iraq that we can not afford to be a crusader to solve the problems of the world, no matter how well intentioned our thoughts are. We have not been elected the problem solver of the world. In Iraq some of the people want us there and some don't and that will be the case in any country to go into. As we know the terrible treatment of humans is worse in Africa and it will be interesting to see what the US does there. Maybe we should just keep out. China beat us there so we may not be welcome. Wherever the US goes, we take guns to bully our cause. Maybe the worst part of US involvement is we don't spend any time truly understanding the local people and what is happening in the area. We keep getting the good guys and the bad guys mixed up. Like in Iraq, we put Saddam in power and then blow up their country to get rid of him. In Cuba the US at first supported Castro and we see where that got us.

We are going to run out of money way before we run out of wars to fight so we had better approach the next war with a lot better understanding of what we are doing than we did in Iraq. Let's go back to fighting terrorism and real threats to the American people. We have given away our jobs and manufacturing and development of our natural resources so how are we going to afford these battles some would have us fight?

Bottom line, America, we are not nearly as perfect as we would like to think we are. I believe most Americans are fine people, but our leaders have been lacking in world wisdom. There is a lot of difference between the average Joe and our elected officials whose main focus is…well I really don't know what their main focus is, but we know what they don't focus on, and that is what is best for America.

Our fathers passed on to us an America that was strong and vibrant and self-sufficient, the manufacturing giant of the world. We were considered one of the richest, most powerful countries in the world. America was respected around the world. Our leaders were known for their wisdom and quality leadership. In our generation we have thrown that all away. The examples are endless as to why this happened. Vietnam, Iraq, giving our manufacturing to China, and poor quality leaders at our national levels. Those leaders were all taking bribes for their votes, each had their own agenda and no one was looking after what is best for America. This type of activity makes a democracy appear unworkable, hundreds of elected officials doing their own thing. It is going to be interesting by the time my kids are old what this thing called American democracy looks like compared to Communist China who after 3,500 years just keeps trucking. They kept going all these years without a lot of money just imagine what they will do now that they are getting all of Americas money.

Chapter 46

Choosing a President

One area of our political system that is becoming more and more out of line is the political system itself. The Democratic and Republican parties both are starting to take on a persona that makes one think they are now the most important governing part of America. The political parties seem to have their own agenda and it is not necessarily what is best for America.

We hear of this or that candidate having experience in the military, in politics, or as an attorney. When do we get someone with experience in economics? A man that truly understand main street economics and knows that you can't go on a spending spree with your military or other government agencies if you don't have the money. This main street economist understands the importance of jobs to an economy and the importance of producing as many goods as you can for yourself. He will understand that the country as a whole has hired him and he will conduct himself accordingly. He will know it is not right to be paid by America and take under the table funds from some group that wants his vote.

People seem to be torn between candidates with political experience or ones with military experience. I don't really want either, the political machinery has lost touch with America so why keep letting them take the lead. A military leader might be our worst choice; I don't think the most important part of America's future is in the military. The president needs to have strong military advisors but to have a military background is not a requirement. One thing a military background gives you is a respect for authority and a love for this country but we need much more than that.

The biggest and most important war we are fighting right now is the economic war, the war we must get into to get our jobs back. If we don't win that war, we won't have any money to pay a big military. So if the current war is about getting our economy back, why not hire a man who understands the economy? Neither Clinton nor Bush seemed to understand that if we give all the jobs away in America it would hurt the economy. I don't know if we have any leaders ready to step up with a deep understanding of this problem. Maybe between now and the next election someone new will step up.

You may have heard of Warren Buffett, one of the richest men in America. We have heard that Warren Buffett only does what benefits Warren Buffett. We need to have a president with that same intensity of economic focus and apply it to running the United States of America. That is what we need, someone who's total focus is America and what's best for America. No pulling the wool over this mans eyes.

We need to find a man like the Presidents of old who wouldn't sell their influence to the highest bidder. Find a leader who would hire informed advisors. Do you see the point? I am not talking about electing a man with a Ph.D. in Economics but rather a man who has proven by his credentials that he understands "down on main street" economics.

I want a president that understands what jobs do for the economy. Bush hasn't understood yet nor do his advisors, so I am not expecting things to change. They won't change so the American people have to change. We have to watch closely those we elect at each election. The most important election is the next one for the President of the United States. Let us find someone who understands the importance of a self-sufficient economy.

The thoughts of President Woodrow Wilson about war was expressed in a book written in 1918 by Arthur Leonard titled WAR ADDRESSES OF WOODROW WILSON.

President Wilson was anguishing over whether or not the US should declare war on Germany.

Germany was being the aggressor throughout Europe and had sunk American ships when they got near Europe and Germany vowed to continue to do so.

Here are a few of his thoughts about war and the position of President of the United States.

"So, my fellow citizens, the reason I came away from Washington is that I sometimes get lonely down here. There are so many people in Washington who know things that are not so, and there are so few people who know anything about what the people of the United States are thinking about. I have to come away and get reminded of the rest of the rest of the country. I have to come away and talk to men who are up against the real thing and say to them, "I am with you if you are with me." And the only test of being with me is not to think about me personally at all, but merely to think of me as an expression for the time being of the power and dignity and hope of the United States."

"We are at the beginning of an age in which it will be insisted that the same standards of conduct and of responsibility for wrong done shall be observed among nations and their Governments that are observed among the individual citizens of civilized states."

"Is the present war a struggle for a just and secure peace or only for a new balance of power? If it be only a struggle for a new balance of power, who will guarantee, who can guarantee, the stable equilibrium of the new arrangement?"

"It was a war determined upon as wars used to be determined upon in the old, unhappy days when peoples were nowhere consulted by their rulers and wars were provoked and waged in the interest of dynasties or of little groups of ambitious men who were accustomed to use their fellow men as pawns and tools."

"If our men have not self-control then they are not capable of that great thing which we call democratic government."

"A man that takes the law into his own hands is not the right man to cooperate in any formation or development of law and institutions."

"We have no quarrel with the German people. We have no feeling toward them but one of sympathy and friendship. It was not upon their impulse that their Government in entering this war. It was not with their previous knowledge or approval."

It would certainly be an inspiration for anyone running for office to read this book. It gives the reader an insight into the humble thought process of wise leaders of the past. They didn't expect rock star treatment that just wanted to do what was best for America.

Chapter 47

What About God

Most Americans recognize that this country has been blessed, blessed by what, some people aren't sure. They know we have been blessed with an abundance of natural resources that until recent years we used as we needed and as we saw fit. We were blessed to live in a country that allowed us freedom of religion, of speech and of job opportunities. Some feel that our belief in God is why this country has been so blessed.

The question of God has came up a lot lately. A small minority of people is suddenly offended that we have reference to God in our schools and public buildings. They point out, there is supposed to be a separation of church and state. No person should be intimidated by any phase of the government to believe in a particular religion in order to be represented by that government. They say it isn't right to reference God in a school because you should then also have reference to Buddha, Mohammed, and every other religion in this great nation.

What we have forgotten on the subject of God, like so many subjects the US is now dealing with, is that America must cater to the majority when there is a question arising about any subject. I have personally meet very few people whom, if they believed in a higher power, believed in anything other than God in a Christian sense.

In a group of 100 people in America if you asked them about their belief in a higher power it would range anywhere from "I think we become road kill when we die"; to "I sure hope there is a God" to "I believe just enough to go to heaven if there is a God", to "there is no doubt in my mind there is a God". In short you would be hard pressed to find someone mentioning any other religion than one that believes in God. Is the name God used in religions other than those that believe in the old or New Testament, I don't know? Apparently Islam believes in just one God and they believe both Jesus and Mohammed were prophets.

In American we have a phrase on our coins or court houses about "in God we trust" but there is no one in our government actively trying to convert you to any religion. It appears that a true separation of church and state is in effect. What that phrase is doing is preserving our heritage. Our founding fathers felt that was an important statement then and I should believe it should still be. Some people believe the statement "in God we trust" simple means you believe in a higher power, no matter which religion you believe in. The new 2007 one-dollar coin has the statement "In God We Trust" on the outer rim of the coin so you have to stand it on edge to read it.

America is known for its religious tolerance. One religion shouldn't force changes on other religions. If I were to move to a country that believes in Buddha it shouldn't be my right to try to have all the Buddha's torn down. That is what is happening if minority religions try to take a phrase off our coins or courthouses. But, if they go into that courthouse and are treated differently from any other citizen they would have a legitimate complaint.

Some people might think it is a coincidence that the countries that have their religious beliefs centered on God are the very same countries that have prospered. America, England and the European countries that had freedom of religion all were blessed with good economies and until recent years all believed in the same God.

· Could it be that those who think there might be a God, or know that there is a God tend to follow the doctrines pointed to in the bible. The Jews follow the old testament, the Christians tend to follow the teachings of Jesus in the New Testament while the Catholics follow a little of each with additional teachings of their own. But all of them have the same common thread of being good to your fellow man; they try to be God like or Christ like.

If a poll was taken in all of America about religious beliefs 90% or more of those polled would accept that if there is a God it is the God known to the Jews, Christians, and Catholics. This is called majority rule. Don't do or say things that would offend our God. In America we try not to offend people with other beliefs and we expect to be left alone with our beliefs in God. If 90% of the American population believes it is okay to refer to God and we have followed a course for 200 years having a reference to God on our money or on our buildings, why are people now trying to change that?

These statements about God are similar in intent to so many other things mentioned in this book, "please leave the majority alone, and in this case leave the minorities alone also." This is America lets not let a few attorneys and their clients bring our parade to a stop by trying to force the opinions of a few onto the majority.

This is indeed the land of the free but freedom comes with responsibility. Individual citizens have a responsibility to pay for their rights by being good citizens. That doesn't mean initiating a lawsuit to try and change something that is part of our way of life.

There is nothing I know of that is a better teacher than joining the military. Within minutes of arriving at basic training you understand, you as an individual are no one, you are part of a unit and it is only the units welfare that is important. Even before the military I wish we all could have had parents that did not tolerate being disrespectful to anyone. Filing a lawsuit to take away a way of life the majority has had for hundreds of years is being disrespectful to everyone, no matter which religion you belong to. I wouldn't think of telling another religion that I want them to remove something from their religious history.

Our individual views should never be forced on someone else. What we believe and why we believe it is part of our own life experience. America is known as a melting pot, anyone who has ever cooked understands how the melting pot works. Each ingredient you throw in soon disappears and blends in with the rest of the ingredients.

We have invited a lot of people into America from all walks of life and all religions, I don't think the large majority of Americans expected us to stop referring to God or stop respecting our flag to please either new comers or those born here. People who have served our country, especially overseas, know the feelings we get when we salute our flag.

To get a perspective of what it is like to cherish America, picture this. You are 18 years old standing guard duty in the middle of the night in a foreign country and you know you won't see America again for 3 more years. You miss your parents, your friends, your old girl friends but most of all you miss America. That 18 year old (me) will die an old man still getting a lump in his throat when he sees the American flag and hears any patriotic song that is played.

At 18 I didn't believe in God, but I didn't try to change religious people. I kept my thoughts to myself. When I was 38 I found there really is a God, but I don't feel a need to go around and convert everyone else to my religion because I understand finding God is a very individual personal thing. I respect a man's decision to not believe in God or to worship in any church he wants. I will respect with dignity any symbols they want whether it is Christian, Buddha, Mohammed or any other religion. I will not try to have them removed from any place they want to set one of their symbols because I am not offended by them. You can worship a rock if you want to, it is none of my business unless you start trying to force your beliefs on me.

You learn when you arrive in a foreign country, to respect the traditions and laws of that country. You try to understand the traditions of the land. When you are a minority you don't start bringing lawsuits to try to change the customs, traditions and beliefs of the majority. The people who are trying to change the traditions of the US are seldom people from a foreign land because new immigrants understand the importance of blending in. A lot of lawsuits are coming from young people who have yet to give anything back to society. They have not yet matured; they have not yet been in situations that bring about understanding, compassion and respect for the rights of others. They have not been around enough to know and appreciate living in America. They still have a high school mentality or at the best college mentality and while we all respect and understand their idealistic point of view the majority of America shouldn't change our traditions, values and love of God and country to fit their point of view.

The ACLU caters to individuals who want to force their opinion on the majority. Unfortunately the majority are not represented in court. Majorities do not hire attorneys to fight back so we are stuck with a lot of the minorities poorly thought out actions and American overall loses more of their rights. From what I have seen in the past it wasn't religious people that were doing the complaining and filing lawsuits it was atheists who didn't believe in any higher power.

I encourage everyone to spend a year "out of country" in any country they want. When they return let's talk about what you found and how you have matured. Go to a country where God isn't spoken of or go to a country where the majority believes in some other religion. When you get to those countries how do you think the people would respond to your attempt to eliminate say Buddha from public view.

When I was in New Orleans I was impressed by a plaque I saw on the Mississippi River just a couple blocks from the French Quarter. That area is called the Moon Walk because it was built 30 years ago, by the then mayor of New Orleans, Moon Landrieu.

"LET US CREATE A CITY WHERE NEITHER THE CHOICE OF RELIGION NOR THE ACCIDENT OF COLOR IS AN OBSTACLE TO OPPORTUNITY AND ADVANCEMENT, NOR A SUBSTITUE FOR EFFORT AND ABILITY."

By Moon Landrieu Mayoral inaugural address May 4, 1970

I hope there comes a day that each person in the United States truly believes that statement is the way we should live.

Chapter 48

The Changing of the Guard

The light at the end of the tunnel in this entire scenario is what I call THE CHANGING OF THE GUARD. I almost made that the title of this book.

For the last 40 years the US has become more and more aggressive. It is using its military might and American cash to bully and intimidate the rest of the world. For some reason we think we are the only country that should have whatever military arsenal we want and we are continually threatening other countries about what they can or can't have. Where we got this attitude I am not sure.

The average American hoped our leaders learned our lesson in Vietnam but apparently we learned nothing so we attacked Iraq.

My fear is that we are about to start WWIII. America is suddenly viewed as the most aggressive and feared country in the world. It reminds me of how the world used to view Russia.

For one reason or another we think it is okay to invade other countries because we are Americans and our intent is always good.

The president we have now refuses to have dialog with places like Korea and Iran and instead prefers to rattle sabers in the news and by the placement of our military. My greatest fear right now is that he is arrogant enough to attack another country. I can see why many countries are trying to build up their arsenal because they think they should be prepared for the day the US decides to attack them.

The last two presidents have proved to Americans and to the world that our leaders lack the qualities to call themselves world leaders. One president gave away our jobs and manufacturing and the other took us to war, what more needs to be said.

Our leaders may not know it yet, but China is no doubt building a military that will put ours to shame. Fortunately our leaders don't know it or we would now be attacking China. China is a shrewd quiet country that is not going to reveal their military until the day they can show us they are powerful enough to beat us at war.

Our fiasco in Iraq may turn out to be a blessing. America has been weakened to the point that we may think twice before we attack another country. We are starting to suspect we can't control the world, especially China, because with them comes Korea.

I keep hearing the phrase "We must stay in Iraq until we win". What is it that we are going to win? We lost and were wrong from day one. I am sorry America there is nothing to win in Iraq.

Bush keeps saying we have to win in Iraq but he still hasn't gotten the picture of what he did to Iraq and America.

America has to be stopped. Our arrogance and military might is all it takes to start a worldwide war. We have been a bully around the world these last few decades. As we know this is in complete opposition to what our founding fathers said America would do in the Monroe Doctrine.

Our leaders don't seem to know yet that America is broke. Between giving away all our jobs and going to war, we are broke. Our factories are gone so a war with China or its allies would leave us without goods.

Had things gone the way Bush wanted in Iraq he would have immediately looked to the next country to attack, like Iran or Korea. I think attacking either one of those countries would have resulted in all out war so maybe the good that is coming out of us losing in Iraq is that the American aggression being stopped short of causing WWIII.

As soon as China steps forward, probably by the year 2010, to show the world they are now the new super power and America is suddenly a distant second, we will officially have what I call the CHANGING OF THE GUARD.

America will no longer be able to look around the world to see who to bully. I just hope when that happens we have a leader in office who understands it is now time to go back to our fore fathers wise advice in the Monroe Doctrine.

It will then be China that will go around the world (they are already in Africa) and be the police dog for the world. The main difference will be it is the Communists turn and I hope they do a better job conducting business than the democratic America did during their reign. From the 1960's forward America became the aggressor whether we want to admit it or not.

I hope China can do a good job. From what I see of what they are doing in Africa, helping the people with good projects, they may not be as bad as what we might imagine. If they become arrogant bullies like President Bush the world is in trouble.

Only a few men run the Communist Party so our future depends on how focused they are on attacking other countries. We are pretty sure their first outing will be to attack Taiwan and America better not step in.

Why has America spent 50 years fighting Communism if in fact they are now good enough to give all our manufacturing and money to? In the Korean War 54,246 American military died fighting Communism. In that war China helped North Korea and suffered the most casualties, China had 967,000 military killed or wounded. In Vietnam America had 58,250 military killed the Chinese supported Communist North Vietnam.

Our leaders must have assumed the Communist China doctrine has changed so much that they are no longer a threat to their people or the rest of the world. We don't know that, do we?

Americans should have a lot of questions for the Clinton/ Gore team to find out just why we allowed the Communist to take over America's wealth and power. Where did Thomas Friedman get such an insight that Communism is no longer a threat?

In this book I have talked a lot about how upset I am that America gave so much to Communist China. I am sure it is a great country with great people and I am one to love and respect everyone. I agree with Woodrow Wilson when he suggested of our enemy, we have no quarrel with these people, our quarrel is with their government.

In history, America will go down with Greece, the Roman Empire and England as countries that lost their worldwide power. Our economy is in the process of imploding and the working class people are out of jobs and history shows us this leads to civil unrest. The people living in poverty are having all their public assistance programs cut back. Our poor are getting poorer and our rich are getting richer, history shows that is a bad combination for any country in the world.

I just hope if we start having a large uprising in our country because of this unrest, another country doesn't invade us and take sides like America has done to other countries.

Chapter 49

Can American Democracy Survive

This book reviews a lot of things that went wrong in the last 20 years. More than anything it has shown the flaws in our Democracy. Yes, we can lose all our freedoms just as we lost being the greatest manufacturing country in the world. Twenty years ago I wouldn't have believed that statement but lets look our government in Washington today. Forget all the hype that we are the greatest country in the world, that is just our opinion and that was yesterday.

The entire system in Washington has been showing us just how bad they have become but we refused to listen. There has not been anything good come out of Washington in years. They have allowed many of our jobs to go overseas, mainly to a Communist nation, they have gotten us involved in a war in the Middle East that never should have happened, they have totally failed on any thing relating to immigration reform. They are continually getting caught in sex and corruption scandals, and selling their vote to the highest bidder. They spend the US dollar like there is an endless supply, sending guns and money around the world and quite often to people that turn out to be our enemy. They have given themselves gigantic retirements, big wages, and have set their own ethic standards. What is so terrible is, we don't even know half the story.

When our elected leaders are on TV it is quickly apparent that they are very shallow and unknowledgeable people. They lack basic knowledge and integrity that would allow them to be leaders with wisdom. They all appear to be very one-sided in their views on any subject they discuss. They spend a lot of their time preparing for the next election, listening to lobbyist and special interest groups, accepting soft money from those people wanting favors and voting for things they may not even believe in, but next week one of the other elected officials will return the favor. They are treated like rock stars for so long they expect that treatment.

Have you ever heard one of our recent elected officials say "Let's do what is best for America"?

They have taken their elected jobs with no training and no understanding that they, as a group, have the ability to destroy our democracy. They don't even try to be accountable because they know they can't be touched.

Washington DC is like a gigantic cocoon filled with all our leaders. The American public can't get in because they have their own set of rules. We can't discipline them because they want to discipline themselves. When they are caught in something they did, they deny it and no action is taken or they admit it and no action is taken.

The total lack of quality leaders for so many years is the hole in this boat called a democracy. Thanks to leaders like Clinton, Gore, and Bush and a thousand other elected officials this great country is now near bankruptcy and no end in sight because these same types of leaders will still be in charge after the next election. This giant cocoon is starting to fester from the inside out and occasionally a seam bursts and what comes out is worse than the last.

If we keep going as we are and try to do nothing to correct our system in 5-10 years America will have imploded and China will be a super power so big and powerful that they could easily take over our country.

We have shown to the world how weak a democracy is, a few decades of extremely poor leadership and it comes apart at the seams. I don't have all the answers on how to change the system but whatever we do we must follow the guidelines of our forefathers because their wisdom is still as good today as 200 years ago. We might start with what this book suggests.

No more money given to our elected officials from any source. Anyone taking a penny or a gift from anyone will be fired on the spot.

Convince our hired officials that America is paying their wage and that what is best for America is more important than party lines.

Make every one of them accountable to the American public under our set of strict ethic guidelines.

Make them sign an oath on the day before the election that if they are caught doing any thing that we have told them they can't do they will resign the next day.

We have to start paying more attention to the intelligence of the people we elect; we have really been getting shortchanged at all positions.

All elected officials have to go through civil servant indoctrination similar to what an IRS or FBI agent goes through that lasts a minimum of one month. The civil service code of ethics will apply to them just as it does every person that works for the government. Those already in office must also attend this class to retain their position.

A lot of our public servants must have their jobs abolished; we have more of them then we can afford. All American workers are downsizing and so must they.

We have to implement changes so that a few people with attorneys can't bring everything to a halt just because they have filed a lawsuit for any reason, whether it is environmental or religious or any other subject.

The people that can bring about the biggest changes to help America are the Wal-Mart owners. There is no doubt in my mind they could bring our jobs back to the USA within two years. I don't think our government will ever act and our businesses won't bring back our jobs without pressure.

I am sad for us, in one generation we allowed this all to happen. When we know what is wrong and don't fix it, we have no one to blame but ourselves. We were wrong, we thought that a democracy could last forever and now we know it can only last if you put quality leaders in positions of power.

We can't even imagine the things our elected officials do that we never know about.

China has shown how to quietly survive for 3,500 years patiently waiting for someone as dumb as the leaders of the USA to give them all our money. I'm not a betting man or I'd place a bet that in less than 100 years no one is going to remember America because China will be so powerful that all other countries will have no meaning. It doesn't have to be that way but if don't change our ways it will be that way.

The people of China and India and other 3rd world countries are hungry to get an education, to get a job and raise their standard of living. Some people think the American people have lost that hunger and would rather not work. I don't agree with that, I think our poor are like the world's poor, they just want to have the opportunity to work and provide for their families. Many of the manufacturing jobs we sent overseas are the ones that our less educated citizens could have had to increase their standard of living.

So much for a democracy. If you don't like what has happened fight for it.

We have to do what we can even if we are without leaders to head the charge.

We let China make the calls for us every time we pick up one of their products.

Right now I think the working class and the poor are on one page and the rich and the leaders are on another. When the stock market crumbles maybe we'll all be on the same page.

In one generation we have shown the world how a few hundred elected officials in a democracy can destroy a country. Now we will see what a few communist leaders can do as world guard dog. If America doesn't change, China will be the power of the future. I just hope China has men of wisdom to lead it.

We still have America and I will be happy if we can save our way of life.

To those people who think it is not possible to lose our democracy read the following explanation as to why the Democracy of Greece fell over 2,000 years ago. Let's see if any of these statements apply to the United States of America.

In 1787 Alexander Tyler, a Scottish history professor at the University of Edinburgh, had this to say about the fall of the Athenian Republic some 2,000 years earlier.

"A democracy is always temporary in nature; it simply cannot exist as a Permanent form of government."

"A democracy will continue to exist up until the time that voters discover they can vote themselves generous gifts from the public treasury."

"From that moment on, the majority always vote for the candidates who promise the most benefits from the public treasury, with the result that every democracy will finally collapse due to loose fiscal policy, which is always followed by a dictatorship."

"The average age of the world's greatest civilizations from the beginning of history, has been about 200 years."

"During those 200 years, those nations always progressed through the following sequence:

From bondage to spiritual faith;
From spiritual faith to great courage;
From courage to liberty;
From liberty to abundance;
From abundance to complacency;
From complacency to apathy;
From apathy to dependence;
From dependence back to bondage."

Professor Joseph Olson of Hamlin University of Law provided the above information.

He goes on to say that 40% of Americans receive their income from the government in the form of wages or public assistance. With the income of the other 60% rapidly declining one can see why the financial situation of a nation can quickly turn upside down. America let's not let this happen to us.

My heart also goes out to each person that lost their job to overseas workers. When those jobs come back home I will also think about those people in other countries that needed our jobs so badly and I can only hope their conditions improve. My heart also goes out to each family that has lost loved ones in Iraq, whether they are Americans, Iraqi or any other nationality.

Whatever religion you belong to pray for our leaders. If you do not believe in any higher power then do what you can to be a better citizen of this great country.

* * *

One more update, it is March 27, 2007 and today is the last day I can edit my book before it is sent back to the publisher.

A couple days ago Iran captured 15 sailors from England and on the news today it talked about how American troops are showing a large buildup in the area. This rattling of the swords is not a good thing. Let our leaders make a phone call to the president of Iran and set down and talk. As I said before I only hope we can get out of that part of the world before we fool around and start World War III.

We have a great fear that terrorists will come into America again and start bombing our buildings and killing our people. Whether or not we exit Iraq that may become a probability.

America citizens that have lost hope and turned to drugs and crime also become terrorists every time they rob or kill. This is going to worsen each year in America as the gap between the rich and the poor widens. Also, the gap between whites and blacks can only get worse when the economy weakens.

There appears to be no end to the consequences of sending our economic advantages to China.

I see the poor and helpless people of America, the children, the old, the sick with no health care, the unemployed and I am just so sad for our people. My sadness turns to anger when I think of this great country going to war and spending 500 billion dollars to destroy another country whose people are like ours, they are just getting by. America has only so much wealth available to spend as we see fit so going off to war leaves so little to help our needy.

Most countries of the world have had war within their borders in this generation. America has been spared that experience with the exception of one day in September 2001, but that was only in a few square mile area. How will we feel if someone attacks our country because they don't like our president or think we have to many weapons and the war goes on for 4 years because the invader can't figure out how to get out of the war?

Chapter 50

Final Thoughts

When I worked for the Federal Energy Administration in the early 1970's the oil embargo seemed to have woke up America about how serious the oil problem was. Our dependence on Middle Eastern oil was causing the US a lot of grief but nothing long-term was done even at that time. The government sent in some investigators (I was one of them) to check on the pricing and production of gas and oil which resulted in some violations and refunds to consumers but not much else happened.

Some people think that after the embargo scare our leaders fell asleep and ignored the problem during the last 30 years, but unfortunately it is worse than that; we went backwards. Since 1970 the number of US oil refiners have dropped due to the fact the environmentalists have done their best to shut down oil exploration in America.

It has been said that the US has enough oil to last hundreds of years but we can't get to it. It is on US Federal land in Alaska and environmentalists have succeeded in stopping oil drilling on that land. This is one of the best examples available of how a few people with their own agenda can stop what is best for America.

With the technical advances available today we should be able to extract oils with very little impact to the environment.

Americans are paying dearly by not allowing this to take place. Buying overseas oil is one of the reasons we are bankrupting ourselves and our dependence on Middle Eastern oil doesn't have to be when we have our own oil.

The exorbitant profits the oil companies are now making lets us know that we can't just turn the oil over to them unchecked, we have to set profit limits. This entire scenario reminds us the importance of finding an alternative energy source. Right now there are several inventions in process that will result in having automobiles and other machinery run without gas and oil. A friend of mine has invented a system that is truly outstanding, but he is having trouble marketing it. By the end of 2007 gas may well be up to $4.00 a gallon with no end in sight. This is becoming a life and death struggle for Americans and this is one of our problems we can solve ourselves.

Remember that we brought this oil price increase on ourselves by giving our manufacturing to China and increasing their demand on oil a thousand times. Attacking Iraq also resulted in higher oil costs. Some writers have suggested that if we pull out of Iraq we may never be able to get oil for America out of that area again. To be effective both of these dilemmas have to be solved at the same time. Bring back our manufacturing and produce our own oil and gas. Whether it is drilling for new wells or alternative energy we have to find a way to separate ourselves from the Middle East oil chokehold they have on the US.

I heard years ago that the US sells oil to Japan as result of some treaty. Is that still going on? The access to gas and oil is so critical to the US I would hope that is no longer the case.

Regarding the fact the Clinton/Gore team set aside 50 million acres of US Forest Service land to prevent drilling for oil and logging, here is the latest word on the effect of that decision.

Yesterday I watched a news report about the insects (pine beetles) that are killing the trees on our National Forests at a rapid pace. The Forest Service employee said that in one 2 ½ million section of US Forest timberland about 1/3 of the timber is now dying from pine beetle infestation. About 600,000 acres will be totally brown and dead this summer and spreading rapidly. He said the fire danger for that forest is severe.

The most apparent question is "why didn't the Forest Service years ago spray to eliminate this insect that is killing our national forest?" When the acreage was set aside by the environmentalist action was that part of the deal, to not allow any spraying?

American citizens own all this land but only a handful of people were able to stop all economic use of this property. The consequence of setting aside 50 million acres of land owned by the US Government didn't "Preserve" it for our children; it condemned it to die by allowing it to go unprotected against the pine beetle.

Terrorism seems to have blossomed around the world after we attacked Iraq. It was like America poured water on a grease fire. If the US was in fact a world leader we showed everyone that it is okay to attack others just on suspicions. That decision also has shown the world that America really is not that strong. A few thousand insurgents are playing havoc with our troops. The world is also witnessing American going broke by both the war and the exporting of our money by sending our manufacturing overseas.

The next person we elect as President is going to have to be a person of extraordinary restraint, wisdom and integrity. He will take the office understanding that the US is no longer king of the world, he will have to try to rebuild what the Clinton/Bush reign took away. I hope he understands that the days of the US trying to control the world are gone. We have become our own worst enemy and we must now take on the job of becoming our own best friend.

The Clinton/Friedman thought process that we are now one big happy world as a result of cell phones, computers and the US giving away its manufacturing has all proven to be false information. America is soon going to be forced to be an island unto itself as a result of our own past deeds. We have spread war, weapons and money around the world and now the world is sick of hearing about us. We are considered bullies and terrorists and nothing more. America is to blame for most of the pollution coming out of China; we should have kept our own manufacturing.

Let's again look around the world realistically to see what is happening. China has become the new best friend of many of the African nations as a result of them bringing in American money and doing good things for the African people. Watch PBS you will notice one very dramatic happening, the Muslims may soon be in charge of many areas of Europe because they will soon be the majority. In the Middle East the total population has a strong dislike for Americans, our attacking Iraq ended any pretense of America being welcomed in the area. In South America the US is not particularly well thought of. The Russians are starting to again not like America (if they ever did). Asia wants our money and manufacturing but they have their own agenda. It is going to be interesting when China finally shows us their new military built by American money.

Where does America fit into all this worldly maneuvering? I think the only place we can fit in is on our own continent. Let us start caring for our own wounded self. Let us think about what we can do to help our own. Let us never again think about going to war against anyone other than an actual aggressor. Let us take a vote of the entire American population before we start another war. If we have to be involved in other countries let it be to help their poor and sick and their economy to make life better for their people.

All over America the phrase "Going Green" is now the buzzword. If you are going green it means you are doing all you can to stop polluting the world to be a part of stopping global warming. You are recycling your paper and plastic, driving fuel-efficient cars, driving less and turning down your thermostat. People are looking at themselves and their neighbors and condemning anyone that isn't doing all they can to stop pollution. Don't forget that anyone that buys something made in China is ignoring the greatest source of pollution in the world; China doing our manufacturing. They are also ignoring the greatest drain on the American economy, China doing our manufacturing.

This book has covered many negative things but hopefully it has also shown you some positive things we can all do to correct our situation. The world is changing and we must change with it, but the change we must make isn't imposing our will more around the world, but imposing it less. Our hearts, minds and money must be turned to providing for Americans above all. The American leaders seem to want to be power brokers both here and over seas. They forgot the little guy in America and they forgot it is not up to them to decide who is in power in any other country in the world. Americans deserve better; the world deserves better. At the next election I hope we can find a President that won't be swayed by cash contributions from special interest groups. We need a person in office that cares for his people and his country more than anything else in this world.

I want to close with one more quote from President Woodrow Wilson almost 100 years ago (taken from the back cover of the War Addresses of Woodrow Wilson):

ONCE MORE WE SHALL MAKE GOOD WITH OUR LIVES AND FORTUNES THE GREAT FAITH TO WHICH WE WERE BORN, AND A NEW GLORY SHALL SHINE IN THE FACE OF OUR PEOPLE.

Chapter 51

The Recovery

UPDATE: May 15, 2009

I asked PublishAmerica to allow me to add this last chapter to my book two years after they published it and 6 years after I wrote it for a very important reason. The current efforts to solve Americas economic crisis has taken a turn that I believe will add to America's decline. Since all my predictions so far have come true I hope my final analysis may also warrant consideration.

I assumed that when Americas economic collapse was finally recognized nation-wide that the politicians would know what caused the collapse and fix it. I pointed out in this book that stopping the harvest of our natural resources and sending all our manufacturing to a communist country was going to destroy America's economy. But as of today, May 15, 2009, no one at any level has suggested to look at these two items as the major cause of our decline. They are looking everywhere for the cause except at what I said would cause the collapse. Since my predications are coming true and none of the leading economic advisors saw it coming I believe my observations are correct.

In this book I said we had until January 1, 2009 to correct what we were doing or it would be to late. The signing of the stimulus package as a way to save our collapsing economy sealed our fate. The almost trillion dollars we are spending to save our economy is being thrown at the final stages of Americas economic collapse, not the cause of the collapse. Think of our economy as a statue, standing tall for 200 years with the legs of the statue being the development of our natural resources and the subsequent manufacturing that it generates. When you eliminate those legs the statue starts to fall. No one notices the statue is starting to fall until they see the arms and the head starting to crumble. When they see the arms falling off they start trying to shore them back up without noticing that the legs are now missing on the statue.

If America does not bring back it's manufacturing I know with certainty that by the end of 2010 the American economy will collapse. That includes all phases of our economy, the stock market, consumer confidence, our government will be broke and tens of millions of more Americans will be out of work.

The experts looking at the collapse are looking at it as if President Bush caused it all. All the signs that I saw were occurring under President Clinton. We have to go that far back to find the original cause of the problem. I feel like the first part of this book covers those events and nothing changes those facts.

We all know that complaining about a problem doesn't serve a purpose unless you can come up with an answer to correct the situation. The following is what I offer to stop the collapsing of the American economy.

THE AMERICAN STIMULAS PACKAGE

The American economy was destroyed one town at time, one mill at a time and one factory at a time and that is how we have save it. Throwing a trillion dollars at a few big companies will have no effect by the end of 2010. Sure it might help the stock market for a few days or months then it is gone. To save the American economy we have to look back at the events taking place on Main Street America. Our people have lost their jobs, our tax base is gone and the money we do have is being spent on goods made in China instead of US made goods. The factories and mines that used to make America rich have been closed; we no longer have any place to get wealth or even to survive.

Can you imagine a trillion dollars being used to reopen our mines, to rebuild our factories, to reinvest in main-street America? We could see some immediate results. The construction in each town is going to bring back those building jobs. The businesses that used to service the factory workers from the supply stores, to clothing stores, service stations, restaurants and grocery stores are going to get to reopen and survive when the factory workers come back. Excitement is all around; America is going to be back to work. Our workers can go home again and save their homes.

A hundred miles away another town that had its factories closed is going through the same thing. Excitement folks, excitement. Thank God someone finally understood that what makes an economy strong is its jobs. Jobs create jobs, value added jobs. Not one-shot jobs that the current stimulus package wants to create. Build a new highway or new school, so what, they are jobs that are gone the minute the project is built. They are being built with government funds that are not going to be replenished year after year.

How many factories across this great country could be built with a trillion dollars? At a billion dollars per factory we know we could build at least a thousand. At 500 million apiece we could build 2 thousand state of the arts environmentally friendly factories that would allow America to again provide for its own consumer needs. Those factories would allow main-street America to again open its doors. The car dealers could again sell cars, the schools would again have a tax base to provide for its own needs, not waiting for a national stimulus bill to have dollars trickle their way. The children in those towns would again be given hope that there will be jobs when they get out of school.

In the 1990's Americans were given the wrong information

about being a nation that no longer needed it's blue-collar jobs. Those leaders didn't have a clue that those blue collar jobs are the single most important jobs Americans can have. Dig ore out of the ground or take wood out of the forest and that simple process creates hundreds of jobs. The product stops at a dozen locations where the ore or wood is turned into a consumer product and at each one of these "Value added" stops jobs are being created and taxes are being paid. This action that starts with the harvesting of our natural resources and ends up in a factory producing a product that ends up in our local stores and in our homes. That action separates the 3rd world countries from the developed countries.

Welcome to REALITY ECONOMICS that does not appear to be taught in the classroom where someone is about to receive his PHD in Economics.

Very little money is created for taxes or to create other jobs when the government is spending it, it is pretty much a one shot deal. But when that money is being spent to bring back the chain that exists between raw materials and individual consumption it is chain that continues to pay taxes and wages forever.

Germany has implemented a program that requires its manufacturers to produce in Germany one half of that company's goods sold in Germany

If the government would rebuild those factories the limits imposed on those companies would have to be strict regarding wages and stock bonuses to the CEO's. The same strict rules would have to apply regarding equal employment without regard to race, color or religion and regardless of union representation. The facilities built could be sold back to the company or leased at a low payment.

While the factories are being rebuilt our mines and timber operations must resume so those factories and mills have the raw products to work with. Our environmentalists must accept the fact they themselves have become one of our countries biggest problems. They brought about legislation and lawsuits to stop harvesting our natural resources and rejoiced when factories are closed without understanding all sides of the story. In the 1990's our leaders sided with them and gave strength to what they were trying to do.

Our manufacturing and millwork is now being done in China where there are no pollution controls. The world now suffers as a result of those decisions because China has become the biggest polluter in the world as they make US products. When this was going on no one was standing up for what is best for America. Closing our mines and factories and sending our money and jobs overseas will go down in history as the most insane decision ever made by a developed country. The worst part is the decision was made by only a handful of people that didn't understand basic economics nor did they understand countries with pollution controls are the countries that should be making our goods.

Automobile manufacturing is now getting its share of the bailout as if shoring them up will save our economy. Are those billions going to get the consumer to buy a car when he still doesn't have a main-street job?

Years ago Americans decided to stop buying American cars, should we look into why that is? Every time the consumer went to a foreign car they were casting their vote against the American automobile. We have all heard a hundred stories about what happened to American auto makers but it comes down to the fact the American car makers fell asleep in the 1980's with their designs. The automobile makers now say the unions were demanding so much in wages and benefits they didn't have the capital for retooling and design. Some say that if the US automakers fail it will collapse the entire American economy. No, the entire American economy is collapsing and the automakers are just one more piece of the statute that is now collapsing. Give the people on main-street back their jobs and they'll start buying cars again, be it American or Foreign. How about telling the foreign automakers that if they want to sell their cars in America then make them in America. Some companies like Toyota are already making cars in the US.

The most important thing in a business isn't whether or not the profits go to a foreign company or a US company (although of course it would be better if it were US) but the most important thing is who is getting the jobs. Are the workers laboring in a foreign country or in the US? Are the products made from goods made in the US, are they coming from our forests and mines or from the ground of another country.

Al Gore was a major player in closing down our mines, the timber industry and closing our factories that were producing some pollution. We see where that got us, a collapsed American economy and the tremendous spike in world pollution as China makes the goods we should have made for ourselves.

The environmentalists that wanted to close logging on our national forest didn't understand that a pine tree has a useful life. Harvest it at its peek, maybe 60 to 80 years and the forest remains healthy. If you don't harvest, the pine beetles kill the forest and you end up not only destroying part of the economy but the forest you thought you could save for your grandkids grandkids dies and goes up in smoke. The environmentalists did not understand the economic value of natural resources. Only the US has the ability to do our required manufacturing while being friendly to our environment. We should not be allowing China to produce our consumer goods while causing extreme worldwide pollution.

HIGH GAS PRICES

In the 1970's when I was an investigator for the Federal Energy Administration we enforced a rule about production and pricing that should have been implemented immediately when the price of gas started going up.

Every time the price of a barrel of crude went up on the world market the American companies like Exxon would immediately price their gas as if they had just paid world price for their oil. But in reality their cost hadn't gone up because they were still bringing oil out of the same American wells. Had the enforcement powers of the FEA been used this gouging wouldn't have happened. The oil companies would have been limited to domestic oil costs plus the cost that they could verify from buying oil at the "world oil" prices. By ignoring basic cost accounting principles, the American gas companies gouged the America public and brought us to our knees all because our Academic leaders didn't understand what was causing the problem. This policy of pricing accountability should be immediately implemented and enforced permanently.

I recently read that the wealth of Exxon now exceeds the wealth of Wal-Mart. In my view that wealth was illegally taken from each American and pricing rollbacks should be immediately enforced. The American public was paying four to five dollars a gallon for gas when it should have never been above two dollars a gallon. You can do the math and see why they got so rich so fast.

Education is not the most important thing in America. The most important aspect of America is, and always will be, that we provide for ourselves. We are the World's leader in innovation but before innovation, is survival, being self-sufficient. We have to be able to make our own steel, our own clothes, our own toys, and our own food because when we provide for ourselves we flourish. In the 1990's our leaders forgot this basic rule.

I have meet thousands of businessmen and most of them didn't go to college, but they are producing goods and giving employment that is the backbone of America. We thought computers and cell phones made us to good to have blue-collar jobs, but we were wrong.

The Chinese don't think they are too good to do our blue-collar jobs and they are now reaping the benefits of taking our money. Their children are proudly going off to work every morning making Americas consumer goods. Most of my friends didn't go to college. They worked in mills and factories and they are now so distraught because those companies have been moved to China and they wonder where their kids and grandkids will work.

Building a highway in Indiana or a school in North Dakota or spending money on a thousand pork barrel projects isn't where the future of America is. Those are projects being paid for by our limited tax dollar and it doesn't replenish itself. In two years we will ask ourselves "Where did that trillion dollars go?" Followed by "It didn't do any good and now we need more government money". By the end of 2010 we will say "My God what have we done to ourselves." America wasn't built on Government giveaways. It was built on sweat, sweat from working and providing for our family and ourselves. The Americans I know want to sweat again toiling for our future, not waiting for a government handout and spending what money they can get on goods made in China.

Remember the phrase "Jobs, value added jobs". This is where America's future is. It is in the increased value when you take a bucket of ore out of the ground and watch how many jobs are created before it becomes a metal chair or a fork. Cut down a tree and see how many jobs are created before it becomes a table or siding for a house. Each one of those workers feeds his family, buys cars and pays taxes. But the real amazing thing is when he gets done doing his job, the product moves on down the line and another American is ready to do his part toward the finished product. That bucket of ore becomes a valuable metal and that renewable resource tree becomes a family heirloom.

China now has thousands of state of the art factories building Americas consumer goods while American factories are rusty and closed. But still our American leaders don't get the picture.

America, the leader of the free world, is collapsing and taking with it the rest of the world as they see America, the big dog, going under. That is a basic rule in any war, when the leader is hit the army panics. This war we are in, we are losing, the economic war.

America changed the dynamics of the entire world by deciding to end its reign as the richest, strongest industrial power in the world. Giving all that money and power to Communist China will forever change the world. Other industrial nations followed our example and shut down their factories to have China do their blue-collar jobs. Now we are all paying for it.

Experts are comparing today's economy to the Great Depression but there is a lot of difference. In the 1930's America was still it's own provider, when the economy did start coming back we just had to reopen our mines, mills and factories and we were on the way the to recovery. What we made we bought for ourselves and everything we did represented American workers and American jobs.

This time around those mills and factories are gone so they can't play a part in our recovery. Our leaders think giving out stimulus money is going to bring back our recovery. In two years we can give away one, two or three trillion dollars and it will make no difference. There is only one recovery program that will work and that is when we once again tap into our own natural resources and we rebuild and reopen those factories we closed.

Government handouts turned the tide in the Great Depression but this time around that will only be a short term fix. In two years all the money we hand out in stimulus to large companies and public projects will have had no meaning.

Before we rebuild our factories we must first guarantee we have the raw materials to produce what those mills and factories need to operate. We have to reopen our mines, forests and factories but the environmentalists have brought about laws and lawsuits that make this impossible. Someone in power has to have enough guts and power to make this happen.

Those few people that brought this on, in the name of saving our environment, have a strangle hold on the American economy. They have choked our economy down now to the point that America is like every other Third World County that doesn't produce it's own natural resources, we are broke.

When we can convince our lawmakers it is time to open back up our natural resources and to stop allowing a few groups to kill this country in the name of the environment, then we can open back up our factories.

At this point our lawmakers must finally be willing to do what is best for America. If the killing of our economy is a result of poor decisions to close our natural resources and factories then we must reverse that. We know with the lobbyists and lack of cooperation by our leaders that will be years off. But we don't have years.

For quick, within 6 months, turnaround lets look back again at Wal-Mart. They can tell their suppliers that in 6 months they want only made in the US items then those manufacturers will have no choice but to bring it all back.

I sent a copy of my book to the owners of Wal-Mart but never received a reply. If you wonder just what America gave away go to that store and pick up 20 random items. I would be surprised if in that group you have one made-in-USA product. Then remember that each one of those items you picked up represents wealth and jobs and taxes to the county that made them (usually Communist China). To the country that buys them (America) it represents the loss of jobs, wealth, taxes, power and it represents the giving away of Americas future.

The average person doesn't know when he picks up a product in a store how many companies and how many employees it took to make that simple product. The simple little product I had on the market required the following lists of companies to be involved. 1. The box company that made the boxes that held 6 of my products. 2. The label company making the product labels 3. The company that made the plastic part of the handle 4. The company that made the metal part of the handle 5. The company that injection molded the main part and assembled it. 6. The company that made the plastics itself 7. the company that made the metal. All those steps and all those companies I used were American companies.

Most of the products you now buy in American stores were made in China so that entire production chain fed the China economy and not ours. Many of these support companies set up shop right outside large factories to have close access to supply their small parts. You can see why opening back up one large company opens up dozens of support companies.

The average American worker that lost his or her job knows the points made in this book are true, but who is listening?

It may be to late for this book to change the course of America but it can be used as a view of what happened to cause the collapse. It was written looking forward but now it is a book that lets us look back and identify what went wrong. Hundreds of economists will be writing books trying to identify our downfall and I just hope this book will end up on the shelf with theirs.

America has wasted its wealth and status to the point that by next year we will have nothing left to squander. What is so sad is that the average hard-working American had to watch helplessly as our corporate leaders, environmentalists and elected officials orchestrated this downfall without realizing what the outcome would be.

When we were a rich country we hired a lot of government workers, but we are no longer rich. Government workers all have the best wages, retirements and health care while the average worker goes without retirement or health care. All the layoffs and cutbacks seem to be hitting everyone but government workers. That has to change because our tax rolls have been eliminated with the closing of our factories and mills so we don't have the money to support this giant public servant workforce. Be it wage cutbacks or layoffs, until we are again self-supporting this has to change.

America is walking away from Capitalism and I don't know where those in control think money will come from to allow America to help itself and help others. Two chapters back in this book we read about the possibility of a democracy collapsing and as we now see America has all the symptoms.

In one generation the combination of efforts of inept politicians, environmentalist and corporate greed brought economic ruin to one of the greatest countries of all time. We showed the world how a few could destroy so many. This should be our lesson that our attempts to force democracy on other countries made no sense at all because we don't have the answers. America going off to war in Korea and Vietnam fighting communism was wasted efforts when we turned around and gave the communist all our money and power. Now our attempt to rescue a few big companies and save the stock market is just a continuation of our leaders ignorance on what makes an economy run.

Some may think the answer is in our Stock Market, invest in it and you'll get rich and America will be okay. In the last few years the market has lost half its value. My prediction is that in the next two years it will lose most of the other half. Most of the companies we invest in have taken their production overseas so those that invested were making money from overseas production and giving overseas workers jobs but not Americans. Neither the investor nor the companies understood that by sidestepping the American worker that our entire country would collapse. Even now as America is collapsing most of our leaders still don't understand this dilemma, they are still trying to figure out how to save the stock market.

The stock market didn't make America great, it was the factories and mills producing goods and jobs that made us the greatest country in the world. It used to be that stock was sold in a company and that money went directly to the company to use it for expansion, or inventory, or remodeling. That is not the case anymore. Most of that money just goes back and forth between traders. It is like gambling, throw money in the pot and sometimes you win and sometimes you lose. When a company issues more stock it is now more often than not stock being issued to its top executives as part of their bonuses. When he then sells his stock it goes back onto the gambling table as others buy and sell the stock without ever helping the company itself.

When a small businessman invests in his company he risks it all. Everything he puts in (which is usually everything he has) is on the line. If he fails he may well end up bankrupt. That is how capitalism works. If it works you may get rich, if it doesn't it can destroy you. With that same thought process some people simply invest in the stock market and hope for the best. They can lose everything they put into the stock market but that is all they can lose, unlike the small business owner that can lose his house, his car and everything he owns. The government doesn't step in to save anyone, the prudent survive his or her risk taking adventure and the unwise fall by the wayside. That is the way our free market system has always worked and I hope we can get back to that sound judgement.

Those people who invested in the stock market didn't do their due diligence; they didn't watch the store. They didn't know their CEO's were making hundreds of millions of dollars a year while they were destroying the company. They didn't know that the company they invested in decided to abandon the American worker and that company would become one more statistic leading to the collapse of the American economy. A former CEO of AGI said that the government never should have stepped in, instead the company should have went to its owners, the shareholders, for the bailout. I don't know which team of public servants made the decision to start taking over various companies but who ever it was doesn't understand what makes a capitalist democratic country operate. Government take over of publicly owned companies has the end result of socialism, no matter what the excuse was for the takeover.

The US Government should never try to save stockholders no matter what company he holds stocks in. It is time to remind investors that they are the ones responsible for what their company did. When the shareholders let it operate in a reckless manner that deprived American workers of their jobs. They invested looking for profit and their risk was whatever they invested. This all should be a wakeup call for investors, the days of easy money are over and so are the days of blindly investing.

Can you imagine what a trillion dollars could do to rebuild America if we simple reversed how we destroyed it? Go back to each individual town that lost their mills, their factories, their livelihood and open up those mills, rebuild those factories and start rebuilding our economy from the ground up. Those people know that is what would revive their hometowns. They know this is the way to do it, not because they have PhD's in economics but because they have a common sense thing called experience. But, alas, our politicians don't look for experience; they want an academic with a Ph.D.

What is really funny about this Ph.D., academic thing, is that it is well explained in the Oxford American Dictionary. If politicians want answers they might do well to read what is said about those Ph.D. experts that are now trying to find a way out of this mess. "An academic l. relates to a scholarly institution 2. Abstract, theoretical, not of practical relevance 3. Hypothetical, impractical, unrealistic doctrine, education without experi-ence."

There you have it. People with PhD's in economics shine in colleges, they are experts that draw graphs and teach theory about how the universe should be run. They can teach or they can go to work for the government but you will never see a main street businessman seeking out a Ph.D. for advice on how to run his business. Private colleges are learning a valuable lesson in their new hiring practices. They are starting to hire the man with practical experience to teach their students all about reality, not theory on any subject.

Not a single academic saw this coming but main-street America did.

With this knowledge, why does every person selected to head our recovery effort have advanced degrees but no practical experience? Talk to the man that had built up a support business that supplied goods to the factory that closed. As a result of the big company moving away he then had to close his company because there was no one to sell his gizmos to. The same goes for the restaurant owner that had supplied the meals for the factory workers that used to live in his town. These people know about jobs creating jobs. The experts that recommended throwing a trillion dollars at the national level to save the biggest businesses don't know about this ground up approach. If the local businesses had survived, the local bank would have survived. If the local bank had survived, his parent bank would have survived. If the workers were still getting a wage, they would still be investing in the stock market. They could still be buying those cars and trucks that no one is now buying. Do you get the picture?

By the end of the year 2010 you will not hear the word recession, the buzzword of the day will instead be "Economic collapse, the American economy has collapsed". When that happens I don't know if anyone in power will even then understand the relationship between the collapse and closing our factories.

THE BANK/HOME OWNER DILEMMA

There are many economic experts today stating the banks and the housing market caused our economic collapse. They think that the ease people were allowed to buy homes and the low interest rate is what brought about America's downfall. Poor people were allowed to buy homes that never should have been allowed into the housing market. That is the reasoning of the experts that offends me the most, to blame this recession on the poor goes way beyond absurd. Let's look further into this housing market dilemma to see if we can find someone other than poor people to blame for the current epidemic of house foreclosures.

Buying a house has always been an American dream and everyone was rushing to buy one, no matter what it took. Banks were in the moneymaking mood and were anxious to lend money just like every other business, but several things went haywire. The boom itself was creating another boom. Values of homes were going up daily and there was a panic to get in on the market before house prices went up even higher. Couples were stretching themselves to buy. By both couples working they could make the payment and everything seemed certain.

Builders saw this buying binge taking place and in places where the market was hot, like Phoenix, Arizona, thousands of homes were being built in anticipation of the economic boom lasting forever. This action by itself was adding fuel to the disaster that was coming. No one even suggested there would be an end to the number of people that would buy the houses that were being built. Now in 2009 there are some areas of the country the value of homes have dropped by 50% in the last two years as a result of the glut of new homes and existing home owners losing their homes when they lost their jobs.

The banks, builders, investment speculators and the American dream of individual home ownership joined forces to create this gigantic bubble that is now bursting. Making the payment on a house was going to require most buying couples to have two incomes. But as the economy collapsed at least one of the couples were losing their jobs because of the economic downturn.

Another sidebar was happening right in the middle of this house buying frenzy and that was the cost of building materials was going up daily. China was becoming the manufacturing capital of the world and they were bidding up the cost of building materials as they had their own building boom. Their boom was more on the side of building factories taking up the world supply of steel and gas.

In another part of the world, in Iraq, materials were being needed in our attempt to help replace what we were destroying.

Even the housing of our troops in Iraq was taking its share of building materials causing the cost of plywood to escalate.

During this time American factories and mills were being closed so more and more of these building supplies were being brought in from other countries. As a result of sending our jobs and money overseas the numbers of people losing their jobs was increasing daily. Each job lost represented another person whose home purchase was being put in jeopardy. As we can now read in the paper daily it isn't just the poor losing their homes, it is people from every economic category. The ones losing their jobs are losing their homes whether they were rich or poor when they bought the house.

That brings us up to today, May 15, 2009. Much of the economic stimulus bailout money is going to help the banks. One would think that in turn the banks would then help the individual homeowners but that is not what is happening. The banks are daily foreclosing on the homes without giving concessions to the homeowners so they can save their houses. Some in Congress are trying in vain to make laws to stop the banks from foreclosure but we hear about bankers having some of the strongest lobbyists in Washington. Unfortunately the average American does not have a lobbyist, unless of course you count the one he voted for and sent to Washington to speak on his behalf.

The basic element of a good person is that when he is helped he will help others. Unfortunately there was no stipulation put into the billions being handed to banks that they must then help the individual homeowners so apparently that isn't going to happen.

It is now being predicted that one in every six homes will face foreclosure. An interview with each of those people losing their homes will indicate that at least one in the family lost their jobs. The job loss will be attributable either directly or indirectly to jobs being sent overseas.

Saving the banks isn't going to save America. What would I

do? I would not have the government step in to save a bank. When the investors in that bank has lost all their money I would then step in bank by bank and buy their mortgages and do a work out with each home owner. Not a penny would be going to a bank investor or bank officer. They were like every other CEO in every other bankrupt business, letting them fail leaves them accountable. This way the owners/stockholders get nothing but their customers, the average American gets help. Local banks never got into this trouble and aren't asking for help.

Had the stimulus package gone into each community and opened back up the factories the local banks, local economy, local housing market could have saved itself.

Businesses started shipping the blue-collar jobs of manufacturing and millwork overseas but it become a wholesale event where even telephone operator's jobs were sent overseas.

So the economic collapse continues. I am still a very optimistic person and feel the current collapse of our economy will turn out to be a good thing. As it said in an old rock song "Times they are a changing".

By the end of 2010 there is going to be a wave of crime like America has never seen. From domestic violence to riots and looting, robbery and murders as our citizens struggle to survive and start losing hope for our future. Our funding for projects to help the average American has already been spent on the military and bailing out big companies. I don't know where the help will come from. The only thing I know that can help is to rebuild our factories and open up our natural resources and do it before it is to late. Oh, one more thing, stop giving our money to bail out the rich and the big companies because the trickle down theory doesn't work. But the trickle up theory will.

America destroyed itself in one generation and what is the saddest of all is that those responsible represent just one or two percent of our population. The politicians, environmentalists and company CEO's for the most part go unnamed and they will disappear into the shadows with their share of the loot and will never take the blame for the destruction they left behind.

I cheer the fact the new president wants to help the poor but each dollar he spends on those in need has to come from those that work. When the workers producing our goods are laboring in another country there are no taxes being paid. With this situation where is the money going to come from to support our government, our military and social security? What about the hundreds of programs developed when our country was rich that all were meant to help Americans in need? If Americans don't have jobs where is the funding going to come from?

It is well said "Not to worry, God is in control" and the saying goes on "Pray for those leaders God has put in office". President Obama I truly believe you are the right man for the right time. You share my love for the poor and it saddens me deeply to see the hardest hit are American workers and the poor that just want to provide for their families. Please help us all.

Throughout history the country that becomes the manufacturing giant of the world becomes the strongest country in the world. That title is about to become China's, the largest communist country in the world. It will be hard for America to give up its role as world leader but that title is already on the way out, we gave it away.

My generation (the Clinton/Bush generation) destroyed this great country and we are the ones that have to fix it. It isn't a matter of maybe or let someone else do the fixing it has to start today. We may now be old men but our children and grandchildren are counting on us so let's go. No more catering to the rich or special interest groups. From now on lets make motto "What's best for America?"

America has become like an old man that gave his fortune to strangers while his own family starved to death. We gave away our technology and we have to buy it back one piece at a time. America created the electronic world but now we have become only the purchasers of the electronic devices, as it is almost all made overseas.

In the next year and a half we are going to experience the biggest economic meltdown in the history of the world. Every phase of the great American dream is going to be shattered, from our savings, retirement, home equity, job security, stock market, our children's future, consumer confidence and even our national security is going to be compromised because our money is gone because we gave it all to China. Our future can only be compared to the decline of the Roman Empire. Our only hope is we still have a choice do our own manufacturing using our own minerals, woods, plastics and fabrics or face the consequences.

There you have it, thanks for reading about the KILLING OF AMERICA.

In 2003 I predicted by 2010 China would reveal the biggest most powerful military in the history of the world and I still stand by predication. China may play it coy and send their America dollars to North Korea and let them be their pit bull but, the bottom line is the Communists will now control the world. In every recent poll the dictator of China is listed as one of the top worst dictators in the world. Do you ever wonder how much of your dollar goes to the Communist Party every time you buy something made in China?

Don't you wish America was getting that money instead of China?

CPSIA information can be obtained at www.ICGtesting.com
Printed in the USA
266864BV00003B/14/P